RELIGION IN IRELAND

321719

Edited by Denis Carroll

Religion in Ireland

PAST, PRESENT AND FUTURE

the columba press

First published in 1999 by
the columba press
55A Spruce Avenue, Stillorgan Industrial Park, Blackrock, Co Dublin

Cover by Bill Bolger
Origination by The Columba Press
Printed in Ireland by ColourBooks Ltd, Dublin

ISBN 1 85607 273 8

Acknowledgements
'A Grafted Tongue' by John Montague, from *Collected Poems (1995)* is used by kind permission of the author and of The Gallery Press. Séamus Heaney's 'Scaffolding' is used by kind permission of Faber and Faber Ltd. The table on pp 72-73 is taken from *Prejudice and Tolerance in Ireland* by Micheál MacGréil, 1978, and is used by permission.

Contents

What's Another Millennium?

Given the 15-20 billion years since 'the big bang', a millennium seems a puny thing. Given the millions of years humankind has been on this earth, one asks what is another millennium? And since many cultures and faiths compute differently (for Jewish people the 6th millennium is well advanced; in Egypt, an 8th millennium has already been ushered in), is not our preoccupation with the third millennium a trifle self-centred?

The year 2000 is not a magical thing. As an enumeration, *anno domini* goes back some 1500 years to when the date of Easter became a major concern of the Christian church. A Scythian monk, Dionysius Exiguus, worked out a system based on the assumed date of Christ's birth. Through Venerable Bede's *History of the English People* that system entered Western consciousness. By the end of the first millennium, there were predictions of the end of the world, the second coming of Christ, a thousand years reign of justice, and so on.

By many evidences, there is a frenzy about 'celebrating' the third millennium – parties arranged months in advance, 'super-bashes', contracts about child-minding, spectacular events, special pay-claims, etc. Yet, one asks, are we heading towards a carnival of waste without parallel in human history? The enthusiasm of the 'Me Too' society to embrace the new millennium may be laudable. Yet, its sheer individualism points to serious problems.

We cannot stolidly ignore the challenge of the time. Nor should we fall into the attitude articulated in Brian Moore's words: 'In the beginning was the word and the word was "No".' If we say 'Yes' to the millennium, what are we in fact saying?

Opting out in sullen superiority would not be counter-cultural or prophetic. It would miss an opportunity for linking millennium to deeper issues of Christian concern. Yet, it is not limited to Christianity – if the millennium is a symbol of hope it should extend to all people, Jews, Muslims and people of no explicit religious affiliation.

Certainly, millennium reflection should not be confined to the business, entertainment and computer world. It should extend to questions of communal authenticity. This is the argument of Gabriel Daly who, in his 'Liberal Democracy, Crisis and the Christian Vision', memorably says: 'In a booming economy few options are likely to favour the poor and it will fall in part to church bodies to keep pointing this out, thereby irritating right-wing economists and governments in power at the time.' Indeed, we have to think globally and take account of widespread hypocrisy in the international community. As human rights activist Tom Hyland puts it, in the global economy there is stress on uniformity; when it comes to human rights other standards apply. Sean Freyne's reminder is timely: 'Millennium talk as practised by the global economy's advertising apostles is intended to divert our attention from the past and present so that it can sell us what we think we need.' Can reflections mainly focused on Irish Christianity help to awaken personal and communal authenticity?

A millennial challenge transcends the interests of international traders and actuaries. It is more than keeping our electronic devices in working order. RUOK4Y2K (Enterprise Ireland's query 'Are You OK For Year 2000?') or America's Me2 ('Me Too For The Millennium') or kindred slogans can be realistic and even necessary. But, taken literally, they are about everything except what Christianity is about – community, love for the other, justice, inclusion, shaping a decent future. They are about everything except remembrance of Jesus of Nazareth. Again, the millennium is about more than parties and 'super-bashes' – with typical good taste one of our foremost poets has remarked that he will greet the millennium in his own bed!

Why a millennium book?

The book here presented is not about dramatic predictions. Nor is it a compendium of wise words about the new millennium. Our future remains open and it is for ourselves to shape what we shall become. If there is an overall 'line', it is celebratory of the 'Christian thing', so formative an ingredient to our society. Hence, the larger part of this book enables the various traditions, marked as we are by historic divisions, to articulate their experience and contemporary problems. Hence Michael Drumm's essay traces the fortunes of the Catholic community in Ireland since the Reformation. Richard Clarke's urbane essay 'On Doing Things Differently' presents the specific contribution of the Church of Ireland and courageously explores the challenges it faces. Bishop Clarke reminds us that 'the Church of Ireland ... is the only Christian tradition which does not have a predominant nationalist or unionist tradition as part of its psyche'. A bracing chapter is written by John Dunlop – 'Who Are These Irish Presbyterians?'; with typical frankness Dunlop challenges the Irish mind to embrace 'inclusivity' in a practical way. In the context of the present peace process, John Dunlop's words are salutary: 'generally, Presbyterians try to get the language right first and then build the relationships ... too much (creative flexibility) may cover duplicity and lead ultimately to the total destruction of trust.' Robert Dunlop, Baptist pastor at Brannockstown, delineates the place of 'minority minority' groups and churches – his call to 'make space' for less powerful Christian voices is both timely and valuable. Dermot Keogh traces the recent fortunes of Jewish people in Ireland. He points up their specific contribution to Irish life while documenting the loss to our society in their decreasing numbers. Joseph Liechty draws on his practical work in ecumenics to trace the legacy and challenges of sectarianism.

While such an 'historical' approach may at first sight be questioned, it is adopted because friendly interchange from diverse standpoints is a significant exercise in mutual understanding. We need it if together we are to contribute to any 'round table' discussion of the future of our society. Even though we cannot predict what the new millennium will bring, we begin to look to the future. To do this, we must pay due deference to past achievements while recognising present 'crises'. Seán Mac Réamoinn's scholarly overview of faith and culture in Ireland tells us much about ourselves, for better and worse. Donal Flanagan's 'lost voices' is an oblique reminder that our Christian tradition is inset not only to our certainties but also to a silent deposit which can still teach us much. Notice how Bishop Walsh emphasises that 'despite our divisions, the Christian churches contributed very significantly to the progress of practically every aspect of civilisation in the West whether in education or the arts, whether in science or engineering, agriculture or medicine'. On the other hand, the book aims to notice shortcomings where necessary, to speak of areas where we all have been 'unprofitable servants'. Notice Gabriel Daly's avowal: 'on the darker side, however, were the abuses of power, and the readiness of Christian leaders to resort to worldly politics and even violence to promote their doctrinal and moral teaching, to say nothing of their nakedly political ends.' In an essay published elsewhere, Fr Pádraig Ó Fiannachta (writing about the Irish language in the new millennium) argues that the real question is about who we want to be – as much a moral question as an economic one. Hence, an argument recurrently made throughout this book is that the Christian churches have still much to contribute in the opening millennium. We are talking of commitment to recovered ideals at a time when ideals are tarnished, inside and outside the churches. Colm Kilcoyne's essay on the crisis facing the Irish Catholic Church rightly argues that if a church can 'release meaning' it will gain, re-gain and keep the allegiance of its people. Likewise, Bishop Walsh's essay, while noticing the many challenges, can suggest that these can be 'in the Lord's own way the occasion which will enable the local church to become truly the "people of God".'

We are talking about ideology, if you like, but not in the sense of dogmatism or oppressive certitudes. Ireland of the late

1990s has entered the global economy. As a result, competitiveness drives out community. Individualism becomes ever more rugged – we have become as determinedly individualistic as the late John Wayne. John Dunlop's contribution (notice the heading 'Back Through Scotland To Jerusalem') raises the question of inclusivity. Can we accept God's universal embrace? Can we recognise that God has many and different children? In Ireland there are very many differences but all are God's children – Catholic, Protestant, Jewish, Muslim, immigrant, poor, unemployed, celebrity, unknown and excluded, etc. Will we accept that God is parent of all these children? Can we see ourselves, whoever we are, as one of these children and brethern to all the others?

At a time of prosperity, can we see the needy as real people? Can we hear the voice of real distress? Now that the problem of emigration has unexpectedly become one of immigration, can we recover a public ethic which respects the widow, the orphan, the stranger at the gates? When we are reputedly 'awash with money' will we seriously address the elimination of poverty in our ghettoes? Will we go along with Seamus Heaney: 'We have experienced a feeling of being called upon, a feeling of being in some way answerable.' (cited in *The Irish Times,* 25.9.1999) Or will we continue weakly to say 'the poor you have always with you'?

In the context of our embattled Peace Process, the churches have to move as well as Sinn Féin or the UUP. The churches would do extraordinary good by shaping their own Good Friday agreement – a millennium gesture – on mixed marriages, eucharistic sharing, integrated education, contested marches. Joseph Liechty's chapter addresses the practical intiatives which can bring much fruit. Likewise, Robert Dunlop's 'Cherishing and Affirming Minorities' valuably invites us to make space for 'minority minorities'. We have indeed progressed from the fearful principle that 'error has no rights' – we need to make a further progression by cherishing all our minorities for the special insights they carry and their ability to bring a fresh voice to a somewhat comfortable consensus. A pressing task is to reach out to those alienated by perceived harshness on dilemmas such as marital breakdown, second unions and homosexuality.

Hopefuly, this book will communicate a sense of hope as well as realism. It is offered as a reason to say that the 'Christian thing' is a gift which we have both used and abused. In any event, it tries to say to reflective people, whether Catholic, Protestant or of another faith/way of life, that 'we are citizens of no mean city'.

Neither Pagan nor Protestant?
Irish Catholicism since the Reformation

Michael Drumm

The story of Irish Catholicism since the Reformation is complex. One must not fall into the trap of equating the church with the bishops and priests; if one does so then all that one will see is the effort of the clergy to suppress pagan traditions whilst fighting Protestant reforms. But there is much more to the story than that. There is the effort of lay Catholics to sustain their traditions in a time of turbulent change.

A traditional religion

The religious system to which Irish Catholics have been attached for around fifteen hundred years might well be termed traditional. What is this traditional religion? One could use other adjectives such as 'folk' or 'popular' to describe it but these terms give rise to pejorative interpretations. When people speak of popular, folk religion they often intend to contrast this with mainstream 'true' religion, the latter functioning as a purifier of the insidious idolatry of the former. When I refer to traditional religion I mean that matrix of beliefs, practices, rituals and customs that constitutes a living religion. Such a religion functions in a very practical way as an interpretative model of human existence and brings together in an apparently 'unholy alliance' the residue of archaic fertility rites, land based rituals, orthodox Christian beliefs and a broad notion of the sacramentality of life. There is much in the traditional practices of Irish Catholics that has not been integrated into any coherent theological framework – just think of fairy forts, holy wells, bonfire nights, ghost stories, pilgrimages, patterns, wakes. All of these have constituted rich data for folklorists, artists and anthropologists but have been largely ignored by Irish theologians. Yet it was these very customs that defined the religious outlook of Irish Catholics for centuries.

One might summarise the lived religious experience of Irish Catholics in pre-Reformation times as follows. There were four great festivals in the old Irish Celtic year: *Samhain* (November 1st), *Imbolg* (February 1st), *Bealtaine* (May 1st) and *Lughnasa* (August 1st). *Samhain* was the festival of the disappearing sun and the other world; the dead returned to visit their people and strange powers were active. This was also the beginning of a new year. *Imbolg* was the festival of Springtime celebrating the start of tilling, the birth of lambs and the return of fishermen to the sea. *Bealtaine* centred on the goddess, imploring her to take care of the cattle now returning to pasture. There were prayers and blessings to protect the animals and for a good harvest later in the year. *Lughnasa* was a celebration of the beginning of the harvest. The first fruits were there for all to see in the last days of July and the early days of August; there was new corn and, in more recent centuries, new potatoes. The earth was yielding its fruit and there was much to celebrate. The fears of *Bealtaine* concerning dairy production and crop failure had passed. The hungry month of July (hungry because the remains of the previous year's harvest were probably already consumed) was over and celebration could begin. People gathered on heights and at springs, made the customary rounds, picked bilberries and wild flowers, danced, played and fell in love, raced and wrestled. They celebrated the land as they looked out over its mysterious beauty. *Lughnasa* was truly a festival of the first fruits of the harvest.

The roots of these four festivals can be traced back to pre-Christian times. But like so many other pagan traditions they were filtered into the life of the Irish Catholic Church. The absence of martyrs in the early centuries of Irish Christianity surely demonstrates a slow evolution of earlier pagan symbols and rituals into a new religious context where they were re-interpreted in the light of the new faith. Thus pilgrimages and holy wells, birth rituals and funerals, blessings and curses, druids and demons, fasting and feasting, continued much as before except that the stories underpinning them began to change. Nevertheless, the elements repugnant to Christian belief showed few signs of abating, despite the best efforts of the clergy to suppress them. Faction fighting, serious abuse of alcohol, lewd games at funeral wakes, raucous dancing at some of the festivals, placation of superstitious gods through fertility symbols and sacrifices, endured. Yet the clergy never ceased in their struggle to suppress these traditions. As late as 1826 Archdeacon T. O'Rorke, commenting on a Lughnasa festival in Ballysadare (Ballisodare), Co Sligo, states:

> The priests of the parish and of the neighbourhood left no effort untried to put an end to these excesses … In 1826 the clergy exerted themselves more than on any former occasion, but they laboured in vain, and in spite of all their preachings and supplications, the patron *(pattern)* of that year was the most numerous and probably the most unruly ever held … The tents were full of guzzlers; the itinerant dealers sold out their poteen and gingerbread as fast as they could receive the price; dancing circles whirled here and there around pipers and fiddlers; ballad singers … drawled out their doleful ditties on highway robbery and murder; mountebanks, sleight-of-hand men, and card-sharpers performed their feats and tricks so as to engross the attention of the gaping rustic … drunken men staggered and shouted, and flourished their shillelaghs; excited men moved about in knots and groups preparing for the fight of the night; … it was a very Babel of noises.

Despite the best efforts of the Christian denominations and the state apparatus, the people clung to their archaic ritual celebrations which probably dated back more than two thousand years. One would imagine that the Protestant Reformation, with its searing critique of image, symbol and ritual, and the Counter-Reformation with its new regulations and disciplines, would have completely undermined these ancient traditions. The reality was somewhat different.

Reformation and Counter-Reformation

If the aim of the Tudor Reformation in Ireland was to encourage most of the people to accept the new ecclesiastical structures then it was something close to a complete failure. Uniquely in Europe, those who rejected the new dispensation were in the majority. Why did the reform not succeed? Certainly the religious houses were dissolved. In travelling the Irish countryside today one can hardly but be nostalgic in wondering about what might have been if the monasteries and friaries had survived and thrived. Think of the books that might have been written, the music composed, the stained class created, the interiors decorated. Instead, all that remains are stone ruins with intimations of what might have been.[1] But nostalgia is seldom a good guide in historical reflection. The monasteries were at the end of a long period of decline when they were finally dissolved. There was little chance of them providing a bulwark against the Reformation as they were more akin to a secular market place than centres of religious commitment and learning. As distinct from the settled monks, the friars provided a more likely source of renewal. The suppression of their houses gave them just the impetus that they needed to become leaders of the Counter-Reformation in Ireland. However, the main reason for the failure of the Reformation was its inability to undermine the traditional religion of Irish Catholics. The Reformed Church in Ireland never had the personnel in terms of preachers and teachers nor the language nor the catechesis nor the commitment nor the cultural insight necessary for a large scale process of evangelisation. Given this reality, and the fact that among the two major subsets of the population living on the island there was little stomach for a church centred on the English nation, the Anglican Reformation was doomed to make little progress.

The most important religious effect of the Reformation in Ireland was the Counter-Reformation. The latter owed its inspiration to the Council of Trent (1545-1563). The Catholic Church had been rocked to its foundations by powerful forces of theological reform unleashed in Northern Europe. The response was aggressive and disciplined but it had little initial impact in Ireland. One might summarise the reforms of Trent as the bishop in his diocese diligently overseeing the priests (properly trained in the new seminaries); the priests in their parishes providing the sacraments in the local church. Thus the pastoral focus of the tridentine renewal was on the parish church as a centre for celebrating the sacraments, preaching the basic elements of the faith and fostering a strong sense of identity.

Such an approach was of little benefit in Ireland where the destruction of church property meant that Catholics had few or no churches to attend. The result of this was a strengthening of the traditional religion described above. The focus of Irish Catholicism became the home rather than the chapel. Mass was often offered in the home and sometimes at Mass rocks; the tradition of station Masses began whereby the priest would visit a townland and the people would gather in a house for the Mass and the reception of the sacrament of confession; even the key rites of passage in Christian life – baptism, marriage and funerals – had to be celebrated at home.

Thus it is easy to see why these believers had to learn how to survive without priests and churches as we know them in more recent times. It was this more than anything else that gave Irish Catholicism its particular flavour. It was a house-centred rather than a chapel-centred tradition for well over two hundred years in many parts of the country and for close on three centuries in other more rural districts. This is why it is probably true to say that the Counter-Reformation could never be implemented in Ireland until there were sufficient church buildings made available and priests to man them. It was only with the mitigation of the penal enactments in the second half of the eighteenth century that any serious efforts at renewal could begin. Clergy, trained in the new Irish colleges all over Catholic Europe and subject to the rigorous discipline of the Counter-Reformation, had attacked the excesses of the traditional practices. In large part, their criticisms of funeral wakes and drunkenness, dancing and feasting, fell on deaf ears. Their efforts at integrating traditional

pilgrimages and festivals into a renewed Catholicism were substantially a failure. The traditional religion of Irish Catholics had
proved surprisingly resilient. But something extraordinary was
about to happen.

Just when the full weight of the Counter-Reformation was
unleashed in Ireland for the first time, in the early years of the
nineteenth century, a programme of Anglican evangelisation
was also initiated with the intention of turning Irish Catholics
into good Protestants. The Reformation and Counter-Reformation
that had hit Europe in the sixteenth century burst onto the Irish
scene in the nineteenth century. The opposition of Protestant
Evangelicals to Irish folk traditions was clear-cut. Here was a
quasi-pagan people placating superstitious gods and seeking to
earn salvation. The comments of Rev Henry M'Manus, a Presbyterian missionary who was in the Joyce country of the Maumturk
mountains in July 1841, are typical. Having described a Mass
that was celebrated at the *Lughnasa* festival, he goes on to say:

> This worship was followed by a sudden transition, character-
> istic in all ages of the religion which man himself originates,
> and which he loves. Amusement became the order of the
> day. The pipers struck up their merry tunes in the tents, and
> the dancing began ... Bread and cakes were abundantly sup-
> plied by peddlers and whiskey flowed on all sides. Under
> such circumstances we may conceive the uproarious hilarity
> of an excitable people. Nor did it all cease till the Sabbath sun
> sought the western wave.

Suggestions of cultural superiority were common amongst
Protestant commentators yet what was really significant was the
perceived effort to convert the Irish poor through the 'New
Reformation'. Relationships between Anglicans and Catholics
deteriorated noticeably from the 1820s onwards. Catholics in
Ireland believed that a new proselytising zeal was evident
amongst Anglican evangelicals, whilst a resurgent Catholicism
in England sowed fear in the hearts of many Irish Protestants.
These tensions ultimately found their focus in the famine con-
troversy over 'souperism', the claim that Anglican evangelicals

distributed soup to impoverished Catholics on condition that they converted to Anglicanism and sent their children to what was effectively the equivalent of Sunday School. People who 'took the soup' became known as 'soupers' and later Irish Catholic tradition used this term pejoratively to identify those who had apostasised and to highlight the great Catholic triumph in convincing most adherents not to 'take the soup'. Opposing Protestant proselytism was a priority for the Irish Catholic Church and explains its preoccupation with the control of education.

The most powerful expression of the Counter-Reformation in nineteenth century Ireland was the parish mission, which seemed to make an almost indelible mark on participants. The missioners – Vincentians, Redemptorists, Jesuits – came from abroad to inculcate renewed theological emphases. They preached hell and damnation, and demanded attendance at Mass and confession. Most of all, they attempted to wean the people away from the folk religion of their homes to the much more disciplined sacramental life centred on the chapel. The first half of the nineteenth century saw an explosion in the building of chapels, with as many as one thousand new constructions. The key pastoral goal of the bishops and priests was to turn Irish Catholics into a church-going population. They achieved this through insisting that Mass be offered only in chapels, so station Masses were suppressed. Through removing corpses from homes to chapels, funeral wakes were undermined. Many of the traditional practices were suppressed and replaced by chapel-centred imports such as novenas and sodalities, benediction and shrines, processions and missions. These devotions were further underpinned by beads, scapulars, medals, missals, prayer books, catechisms and holy pictures. By 1870 the Counter-Reformation was triumphant. The census returns of 1861 proved that the efforts of Protestant proselytisers were essentially a failure and the great mass of the Irish people were practising Catholics. The new spirituality assumed the high moral ground of the respectable middle-class, rejecting the raucous religion of an earlier time in the embrace of individual rigour, personal scrupulosity and sexual abstinence.

It is indeed extraordinary that the powerful forces of Protestant proselytism and Catholic renewal were simultaneously unleashed in Ireland around the beginning of the nineteenth century. But both of them pale into insignificance alongside the most tragic event in Irish history which was about to unfold in the 1840s. Undoubtedly both of these tendencies capitalised on the Great Hunger of the 1840s in their desire to further their goal of purifying Irish Catholics of their quasi-pagan instincts. By the end of the century, the traditional religion was little more than a folk memory.

The Great Hunger

But the psychological, religious and political implications of the Famine went much deeper. The Famine changed everything and facilitated the emergence of that pious individualism which is so characteristic of late nineteenth and twentieth century Christianity. Between 1845-48 the world of the poor Irish peasants ruptured and died; there were no new potatoes to celebrate at *Lughnasa* time and the ancient traditions must have seemed empty in the face of such a calamity. As, centuries previously, the Black Death had changed the religious consciousness of Europe, so the religious mind and heart of the Irish peasantry would be transformed. It is in this sense that it is probably true to speak of contemporary Irish Catholicism as a post-Famine phenomenon. One might analyse its effects under several different headings.

Suppressing the Memory

One of the key insights of contemporary psychology is that people suppress the memory of great traumas in their individual lives. Similarly Irish people suppressed the memory of the Great Famine. When one begins to delve into the enormity of the horror that was unleashed, this is easy to understand. The Irish Famine is one of the great disasters of peace-time history. In the aftermath of famine there are no good stories to tell. Rather the chances are that the main stories are of neglect, cheating, stealing, gaining on the backs of others and the ultimate horror – cannibalism. This is not the stuff of songs and fireside storytelling. In famine it is impossible to identify the enemy and so heroism is difficult to describe. It is easy enough to identify the hero in the face of colonial occupation, but what is heroism in the face of blight? Who were the heroes – those who died? those who emigrated? those who survived at home?

The latter group gained as a result of the Famine and one can legitimately speak of a survivor complex. It seems almost too obvious to remark upon but it is worth reflecting on the fact that the people who now live in Ireland are the descendants of those who survived the horror of famine; the majority of their forebears did not die or emigrate. In reality the gains in the medium term for those who survived were hugely significant economically, socially and politically. It seems plausible to surmise that they might indeed repress the memory of the Great Hunger, and in this their behaviour is clearly distinct from the Irish of the diaspora. Folklore traditions amongst the native Irish relating to the famine are scarce, whereas the famine remained one of the great themes in the lives of the Irish of the diaspora. Here is a simple example: ask Irish Catholics living in Ireland to analyse the historical causes of the troubles since 1969 and they will speak of plantations and Cromwell; ask the same question in Irish Catholic working-class areas of Liverpool or Boston and one will almost invariably hear of the Famine. The ultimate demonstration of suppressing the memory was the centenary years of 1945-48, when the neophyte state all but ignored the events of one hundred years earlier. Why do we now recall the Famine one hundred and fifty years later? As ever, historical distance has opened up more space to reflect. Poets, dramatists and historians have given us language, images and analysis to think through the horror. Missionaries and aid workers encountered famine anew and their contemporary experience has retrieved a long lost memory in the Irish psyche.

Surviving the consequences

People and institutions adapt and change in the midst of overwhelming catastrophes. The Irish Catholic Church was rocked
to its very core by the events of the 1840s and not least by the
widely held belief that Anglicans and Presbyterians had used
the tragedy for their own purposes. The Catholic Church, under
Paul Cullen's leadership and with the outstanding contribution
of the new religious orders, responded aggressively. Education
and health care provision became key pastoral goals in Irish
Catholic communities throughout the world as people sought to
protect themselves against future horrors. The explosive numbers who entered seminaries or joined religious orders meant
that there was a very large and talented pool of people available
to provide badly needed pastoral services. Whether in Belmullet
or Brooklyn, Cricklewood or Cape Town, Limerick or Lagos,
Irish priests, brothers and sisters pursued the same pastoral
strategies from the 1850s until the 1960s. At home, Irish
Catholics began to build – churches, presbyteries, hospitals,
schools. For a people bereft of buildings for centuries these new
constructions became an important symbol of their faith. Even
down to today, one will hear the complaint that Irish clergy are
preoccupied with church buildings to the neglect of more important pastoral issues. But one shouldn't lightly dismiss the
psychological importance of these new buildings that sprouted
up all over the country in the latter part of the last century. At
least one Catholic would live in a house to vie with the local
landlord! And so the Parish Priest's house was a rather large
construction for a single, celibate man.

The landlords never really recovered from the Famine. The
tenant farmers grew in stature throughout the second half of the
nineteenth century and, along with the newly emerging Catholic
middle-class, became the foundation of the newly independent
state after 1921. Throughout this time, the bishops and priests
were preoccupied with education – some, no doubt, because
they saw it as the long term key to political freedom and a decent
livelihood for their poor people, others because they wanted to

control it at all costs. This division ultimately suited both groups – the lay Catholic middle-class took over the levers of political and economic power while the clergy and religious orders dictated the agenda in education. The newly founded state after 1921 buttressed this division of power.

The consequences of the Famine were evident in all spheres of Irish life but probably nowhere more clearly than in attitudes towards sexuality. After the Famine people married later in life, and many never married at all. The Catholic Church preached a message of temperance and sexual abstinence. As was noted earlier, the newly emerging Catholic middle-class rejected the raucous religious expression of an earlier age in the embrace of personal scrupulosity, individual ambition and religious rigour. The latter was facilitated by frequent recourse to the sacrament of confession whilst the dominance of Victorian values in a wider context reinforced an atmosphere of sexual repression. In the aftermath of terrible famine, it is not difficult to link sexual expression and guilt; celibacy and sexual abstinence would have emerged as socio-economic as well as religious values. Sexual experience and guilt feelings appear to be linked in different ways but one must surely regret the oppressive ethos of sexual repression so characteristic of post-Famine Irish life.

Hunger stalked the land of Ireland many times in the nineteenth century; most shockingly of all it revisited the people of Connacht thirty years after the Great Hunger in the late 1870s. In 1879 the poor of Mayo were in a wretched state, there was nothing to celebrate around *Lughnasa* time as the potato crop failed. On August 21st, several people claimed to see a Marian apparition on the gable wall of the church in Knock. Michael Davitt's land war was about to begin and the word 'boycott' would soon enter the English language. Yet again the complex identity of Irish Catholics was manifesting itself.

Characterising Relationships
Relationships between Irish Catholics and Protestants have always been fraught but probably hit their lowest ebb in the im-

mediate aftermath of the Famine. There have been sectarian
riots on the streets of Belfast in every decade since the 1840s, the
claims concerning 'souperism' poisoned relationships in many
local communities, and it is only since the 1960s that a real dialogue has commenced. There is deep suspicion between the
Christian communities in Ireland over land, nationality and
colonialism. The wounds of history are deep. The imagination
still bears the scars of the Famine that was endured, the land that
was fought over and the language that was suppressed. Famine,
land, language – could one think of greater forces for forming
the imagination? It is hardly surprising that feelings of inferiority
and pain are so much a part of Irish Catholic consciousness. The
great danger with an inferiority complex is that one withdraws
into a ghetto, smugly secure with one's own certainties concerning the hostile world outside. Unquestionably Irish Catholicism
gave way to this temptation, so that as late as the 1950s one finds
the best minds of the Irish Catholic Church dealing with questions such as attendance at services in Protestant churches, state
regulations concerning dances, and endless minutiae relating to
liturgical rubrics.

But there is another relationship that might prove even more
important in the longer run – the relationship of Irish Catholics
to the enlightenment consciousness of the modern world. The
conventional wisdom of the liberal media/academic establishment in contemporary Ireland is that Irish Catholics were held
in bondage for centuries by an oppressive church and that only
with open access to education since the 1960s have people begun
to escape the clutches of this all-powerful institution. I believe
this form of analysis to be fundamentally flawed. As a simple
all-embracing hypothesis it is very attractive, but such all-embracing hypotheses are almost invariably false. What alternative
explanation might one offer? This paper has suggested that we
have failed to give sufficient weight to the effect of the Great
Hunger of the 1840s on Irish Catholic consciousness. The enlightenment did not influence Irish Catholics because the Famine
had turned their hearts and minds in a different direction – not

towards the rights of the individual, freedom of enquiry, respect for the emerging sciences and progress; but towards survival, tenant rights, emigration and fear of what life might hold. It took generations to come to terms with these issues. As a result there is an extraordinary coincidence in Ireland in the 1960s of modernity (in terms of the beginning of industrialisation, urbanisation and secularisation) with the Second Vatican Council. Just as modernity was beginning to doubt its own values, both Ireland and the Catholic Church were embracing it for the first time. For Irish Catholics it was a time of overwhelming change. What the long term results will be, it is still too soon to say.

Conclusion

Great historical forces have shaped the religious consciousness of Irish Catholics. Over the centuries, Christian and pagan practices formed a vibrant pre-modern expression of religious belief. The Great Hunger of the 1840s and the forces that it unleashed gave a particular flavour to Irish Catholicism. Only since the 1960s has this pre-modern mix of faith and culture hit the rocks of modernity. Naturally this has given rise to a certain shapelessness as the icons of an earlier time came under sustained critique. Different groups and individuals will respond in varied ways to this critique. In analysing these responses, a few pointers from the past appear particularly apposite.

(I) The individual's search for meaning is not a good lens through which to read Irish Catholicism. There is little attention given to secular humanism, nor even to philosophical reflection, in this tradition. It is not a religion of ideas but of lived encounter with the community, the earth and the forces of the beyond. This encounter is expressed through rituals and symbols which are both Christian and pagan. At times the paganism of these expressions will offend the sensibilities of the learned – the most recent example being the popular interest in moving statues of the Virgin Mary. Those who prefer a more modern, intellectual approach to religious faith find in these practices everything that is objectionable in traditional Irish religiosity: superstition,

magic and a preoccupation with strange powers. But what is
most questionable in this rich tradition is a failure to link an extraordinary interest in rituals and symbols with morality; it is as
if the rites in which people participated were more of an escape
from reality rather than a challenge to face up to moral responsibility. This led the clergy to preach a very strict moral code
over the last couple of centuries. The collapse of this code has
encouraged many contemporary commentators to wonder what
moral underpinning remains once one removes the strictures of
the clergy.

(II) Irish Catholicism is a communal reality, both for good
and for ill. The most significant expressions of this identity became the rural parish (copper-fastened by its links with the
Gaelic Athletic Association) and the funeral celebration. In these
and other contexts it was clear that the individual was not alone
but that there was a living community. Of course, others found
this same community grossly invasive of their privacy and very
unforgiving if one opted out of its defining mores. As a society
evolves from valleys of squinting windows to cities of bleak
anonymity, it is difficult to predict how a religious faith predi-
cated on communal interaction will adapt to such a changing
scene.

(III) Irish Catholics have itchy feet. With the exception of the
Jews, probably no people has travelled so much. From the remarkable peregrinations of the monks of the early Irish church
to the military flights of earls and geese, from the forced emigration of the last two centuries to the missionary outreach of this
one, millions of people have moved and settled in new homes. If
these people were traditional in their religious outlooks they
certainly were not conservative, as they managed to adapt to
varied economic, environmental and political contexts. Those
who stayed at home, so to speak, went on pilgrimage. Whether
to the mountain or to the holy well, to the saint's bed or to the
Marian shrine, there appeared to be an insatiable appetite for
pilgrimage. These pilgrimages were not an escape from life but,
as the two most famous centres – Station Island on Lough Derg

and Croagh Patrick – amply demonstrate, an encounter with the reality of struggle and pain which could not be avoided. The itchy feet are not just geographical but also spiritual. The people drank from many different spiritual wells over the last fifteen hundred years. Who knows what wells they may drink from in the future?

(IV) The high tolerance level that Irish Catholics have for their clergy is notable. As a result, there has never been any major popular expression of anti-clericalism. Maybe it is because Catholic priests inherited much of the powers of pre-Christian druids and were bestowed with the mystique associated with sacred figures who offer sacrifice in all traditional religions. Maybe it is related to the persecution of some clergy in the sixteenth and seventeenth centuries. For whatever reason, the priest was held in high regard. This respect survived even the most glaring abuses of power, scandalous avariciousness on the part of some, and myriad other misdemeanours. It also helped the people to cope with changes in pastoral practices. There are many examples of these changes but probably the best is the story of the Station Mass. In the eighteenth century the priest visited particular homes before Christmas and Easter to provide the sacrament of confession and to say Mass. Over time this became a strong element in popular Irish Catholicism. But with Cardinal Cullen's desire to transfer all religious celebrations from the home to the chapel, a process of suppressing the house stations was started by the clergy in the mid-nineteenth century. In most of the country they disappeared but in some places they survived just long enough to reach the Second Vatican Council after which the clergy re-discovered the significance of the house Mass and put much energy into reviving it. Such are the vagaries of clerical preoccupations. The people discovered that when it comes to liturgical and sacramental issues, it was best to put up with what the priest said because it was quite likely that his successor would say something very different. Thus a debilitating passivity and inertia became the liturgical norm. Even today, believers are very tolerant of liturgical and other defects.

It is, of course, an open question whether this toleration of clerical limitations will survive the revelations of the 1990s.

(v) Is it true to say that Irish Catholicism is neither pagan nor
Protestant? Is it not more true to say that its inheritance today is
both pagan and Protestant? Pagan – in that some believers are
still attracted by traditional forms of religious expression;
Protestant – in that some of its adherents have embraced core
values of the Reformation like freedom of conscience, the rights
of the individual, challenging authority, questioning many
traditions. The future promises to be as complex as the past.

Notes:
1. cf. Donal Flanagan's 'Lost Voices', pp 127-139.

On Doing Things Differently:
A Church of Ireland glance at the past

✠ Richard Clarke

When it comes to the church, the past is far from being another country. Indeed, how a particular ecclesial community interprets its history may be as valuable for the purpose of discerning its future potential as in understanding its present idiosyncrasies. It is therefore of more than a little significance that the Church of Ireland has, within the past generation, undergone something of a sea-change in its assessment of its own place within Irish history. It is probably fair to say that until the nineteen-sixties, the self-understanding of the Church of Ireland, north and south, was that it was the only real and legitimate heir of a Celtic and Catholic church that had blossomed in the time of St Patrick. It had recovered this tradition at the time of the Reformation and, although it had been somewhat tarnished by associations with the established national church in England, the Church of Ireland was nevertheless an entirely Irish church, fully entitled to its title. Furthermore, most of the criticisms levelled at its behaviour over the centuries since the Reformation were the result of the wicked propaganda of Roman Catholic and dissenter alike.

A general acceptance within the Church of Ireland today that such an interpretation is in most respects a grotesque distortion of reality (to put it mildly), is in part the consequence of the comprehensive revolution in the methods and motivations of Irish historical research, but it is more. It is also, I believe, the result of a growing understanding that within the Church of Ireland we can and must live with the untidinesses and corruptions of our own history if we are to have any future. Of course we will still carry cherished fantasies as part of our cultural baggage. Every institution, ecclesial and non-ecclesial, will do this to preserve its own self-confidence. Is it too much to believe that little by little the fantasies of all the churches will encompass less triumphalism and more self-criticism? Perhaps the Church of Ireland General Synod of 1999 showed glimmerings of a reluctant willingness to face the tyranny of our past with some honesty. What follows within this essay is far from being a chronological continuum of the history of the Church of Ireland through to the present from our chosen starting point in the renaissance and Reformation, the traditional genesis of the post-medieval period. Even less is it an apologia. It is instead a highly individualistic view (in which there may well seem to be huge omissions) of how aspects of our past have served to shape the culture of the Church of Ireland we see around us today.

Our set starting block, the Reformation, was itself far from neat and systematic. It came in consequence of a nexus of bewildering changes throughout western Europe as a new intellectual culture, accelerated by the new technology of printing, spread rapidly. Learning and thinking were no longer the preserve of the church, nor was an assured place within the political hegemony. Inevitably, changing thought patterns produced new spiritual thinking. It is certainly true that the Anglican Reformation had, as its catalyst, political considerations in the deteriorating relationship between an anxious English King and a far from independent Pope. Yet, it would be more than foolish to imagine that this Reformation would have happened without the wider context of the Reformation in Europe as a whole. Doctrinally, the Anglican Reformation was extremely conservative, particularly in its early stages. In Ireland it was also a very patchy operation. But it would again be unwise to accept the traditional assumption that only a diminishing area of English influence was affected by the Reformation, or that it encompassed no continuity with the past. When, at the beginning of Elizabeth's tenure on the English throne, following on the brief reign of her Catholic half-sister Mary, an Act of Supremacy was passed, and later Twelve Articles of Religion were constructed in line with Reformed thinking – both the Act and the Articles requiring subscription by bishops and clergy – most seem to have done so, although relatively few of these would have been of English name or background. This does not of course mean that the Reformation actually 'took' throughout Ireland. That would be to read back twentieth-century notions of the nation-state and the nature of society into a totally different setting. Things were far less tidy and far more complicated than that. If we ask the question as to how the Church of Ireland today looks at its Reformation heritage, there is also a great deal of untidi-ness. There may even be a degree of schizophrenia.

To understand this we probably need to leap over three hundred years from the sixteenth-century reformations to the disestablishment of the Church of Ireland in 1869. It is a point to which we will return later, but at this juncture it should be noted that from the time of disestablishment, relationships between the Church of Ireland and the Church of England (which had technically been a single church only for the seventy years be-tween the Act of Union and Disestablishment) soured and have never totally sweetened since. The Church of Ireland felt be-trayed and abandoned by a sister church, and it is probably fair to say that since then, the Church of Ireland has always (even if not always consciously), kept its distance from the Church of England. An Irish sense of Anglicanism is far from being a sense of Englishness, and this is not merely a southern Irish perspec-tive. Even among those members of the Church of Ireland who would have a very strong perception of being British, the Church of England is emphatically not a mother church to the Church of Ireland. This point is perhaps best symbolised in the current practice of a close and growing relationship between the bishops of what is sometimes affectionately called the Celtic fringe. The Anglican bishops of Ireland, Scotland and Wales meet regularly, but separately from the bishops of the Church of England. And so there is a dichotomy. There is, on the one hand, a strong sense of being part a reformed church within the Anglican tradition. On the other hand, there is a singular reluc-

tance, regardless of political viewpoint, to be over-associated
with the particular church that was the progenitor of the process
of reformation in these islands.

Moving from the Reformation to another decisive moment
within the life of the Church of Ireland, we may advance for-
wards a century to the Rebellion of 1641. This was indeed a
watershed in relationship between Ireland and the Church of
Ireland. For as long as a general ecclesiastical and political un-
tidiness remained, there was an inevitable overlap and ambiguity
in the relationship between the different ecclesial groupings
(and even the notion of ecclesial groupings is something of an
anachronism). And so, although the early seventeenth century
settlers in Ulster were for the most part 'Presbyterian' (or at any
rate Calvinistic in theological outlook), the lack of definition in
much of the Church of Ireland's doctrinal position at this point
meant that many of the settlers were somehow assimilated into
the 'Established' Church of Ireland. This occurred without any
attempt to ensure a conforming even to some of the basics of an
Anglican ecclesiology, as represented for example by its *Book of
Common Prayer* or its system of episcopacy. As the period also
marks a time when the church was being neglected by its own
leadership (with few glittering exceptions, the most notable of
whom would be the famous Bishop Bedell) and parishes were
falling into spiritual ruin and churches were falling into physical
ruin, it was not, from the church's point of view, the best time
for political upheaval. However, the dissatisfaction of the 'Old
English' (those who were the descendants of the English families who had settled in Ireland before the Reformation and had
remained loyal to the Roman Catholic Church) with the vacill-
ation of Charles I and his advisors, brought them into a new
coalition with those who had never had any love for the English
and who had indeed been thrown from their lands by the systematic plantation of Ireland.

Inevitably the Church of Ireland was a target from all sides.
If, from the perspective of over three and a half centuries' distance, it is hard to empathise with the Church of Ireland in that

period, that is (for the purposes of this essay) of little relevance. What is of consequence is that from this point, the Church of Ireland began to take upon itself the mind-set of a garrison – albeit not necessarily for the English. Indeed, Cromwell had no more love for the Church of Ireland than for Irish Roman Catholics, and the Church of Ireland at the Restoration in 1661 had to take on a major task of reconstruction. As this reconstruction involved a forceful regularisation of the relationship with Presbyterianism, the garrison now felt itself unloved by every other religious tradition on the island, not without good reason. But that aura of defensiveness, if not outright paranoia, may still be sensed today.

And yet the period of the Restoration – the conclusion of the Caroline age – has also had its lasting influence in a very different way. The Carolines, of whom Jeremy Taylor and John Bramhall were probably the most illustrious, recalled the Church of Ireland in particular and Anglicanism in general, to its sense of being both Catholic and Reformed. That summary of the Carolines has very often been used as a piece of mindless triumphalism (with a sub-text that implies the inherent superiority of Anglicanism over other Christian churches) but at its heart it is more than that. It demands that the church live with a tension between its poles of Catholicism and *reformata sed semper reformanda* (reformed but always in need of reformation), and insists that it denies either aspect of its inheritance at its peril. In the context of Anglican theological exploration and ecumenical dialogue, the Carolines have, in the late twentieth century, come into their own again. The earlier Anglican-Roman Catholic International Commission documents evoked the spirit of the Carolines to a considerable degree. Although it cannot in honesty be suggested that the Church of Ireland as a whole is today redolent of the spirit of classical Caroline Anglicanism, it is good to note that much of the re-assertion of the Carolines for our generation may be attributed to an Irish Anglican, the late Henry MacAdoo, one-time co-chairman of ARCIC. And there should be no doubt that it is in the Carolines that an honest convergence between the Roman Catholic and Anglican churches must be sought.

Given that King William III and the mantra of 'Remember 1690' seem to have become the touchstone for religious divisiveness in one part of Ireland today, where does William fit into the culture of the Church of Ireland? It would be very easy simply to airbrush him out of the picture, but that would be less than honest. In that there is no doubt but that King James would undoubtedly have replaced the Church of Ireland by the Roman Catholic Church as the church of the country, it is clear where Church of Ireland (and indeed all Protestant) sympathies would have been. Ironically, of course, the Pope was more than a little ambivalent as to whom he would have wished to have secured final victory in the war between William and James, given that James had been given the support of the French, but that is now only one of the delightful ironies of history. The aftermath of the Williamite victory was a period of ascendancy in every sense of the word for the Church of Ireland.

Two aspects of the eighteenth century have shaped public perceptions of the Church of Ireland through to the present day. The first is that the upper ranks of the church in the eighteenth century appeared to be, for the most part, the preserve of idle and careless English clergy who spent as little time in Ireland as possible. This is something of an exaggeration and had in any case changed radically by the early nineteenth century, but somehow the critics of the Church of Ireland did not change their minds as speedily. The second stigma of the Church of Ireland in the eighteenth century was the legislation known bleakly as the penal laws. The days of the penal laws were indeed shameful and if they were 'of their time' and not so much specifically anti-Irish as designed for the preservation of privilege in 'a Protestant kingdom', the legacy of those years in terms of attitude towards the Church of Ireland are undoubtedly a matter of acrimony to this day. There can be no evading the truth that the intention of the penal laws was to bring the Roman Catholic population into subjugation.

When we move into the nineteenth century we find a more concerted attempt to bring the Roman Catholic population into the Church of Ireland, a very different matter. The early decades of the nineteenth century were a time of evangelical zeal in every direction for the Church of Ireland. There was a new interest in missionary work in other countries, but conversion was to begin at home. There was hope that there would indeed be 'a second Reformation' and although little permanent resulted from the efforts of the evangelists, the association of proselytisation with the response of the Church of Ireland during the terrible years of the Famine has led to that single epithet 'souperism' retaining a power to the present day. As with so much else, there are good reasons to apologise for the Famine (although whether one may legitimately apologise on behalf of others is less certain), and there are also good reasons to contextualise. In the case of the Famine there are instances of sacrificial and costly service on the part of members of the Church of Ireland. Sadly, balance in the matter may not be the issue today. The Church of Ireland is having to live with an aspect of history that contains much that is unpalatable. Perhaps one of the most constructive perspectives a couple of years ago, at the one hundred and fiftieth anniversary of the nineteenth-century Famine, was the insistence that together, as a country, we look at those today whose famine is now the responsibility of all of us in the developed world.

Through the nineteenth century, the Church of Ireland's sense of the importance of evangelisation and mission was paralleled by the realisation that its days as the privileged and established church of the country were numbered. From the eighteen-thirties onwards, it was becoming clear that it was only a matter of time before the privileges were taken from it. At the same time, the Roman Catholic Church in Ireland was becoming more confident and, under Cardinal Cullen, more centralised, organised and visible. One of Cullen's achievements was to ally the Roman Catholic Church with the moderately nationalistic National Association. The effects of this were to make Roman

Catholicism coterminous in the popular mind with Irishness. This was a new development and I would wish to contend that nothing has been more disastrous for either the Roman Catholic Church or for the other churches. Nationalism (certainly as we understand it today) is at heart a nineteenth-century invention, and it would never have been considered intelligible to have thought of Irishness in such narrow terms until the mid-nineteenth century. However, members of the Church of Ireland (and the other reformed churches) have since that time had to live with the unwarranted accusation that they are not Irish because they are not Roman Catholic.

And at the height of the Cullenisation phenomenon, there was a further circumstance that has undoubtedly left an indelible mark on the mind-set of the Church of Ireland, viz. the disestablishment of the church in 1869. I have already mentioned the ambivalence in relationship with the Church of England resulting from disestablishment. But within the Church of Ireland a entirely new mentality developed with disestablishment. The sober truth is that the church came very close to disintegrating at disestablishment. The cause was not financial nor even political, other than in a derivative sense. The fact was that the Church of Ireland was a divided church in terms of doctrinal stance and what is loosely called churchmanship. All the tensions between what was meant by Catholic and what was meant by Reformed came to the surface in the years immediately following disestablishment, as debates (particularly those on the revision of the *Book of Common Prayer*) in the newly formed General Synod amply demonstrated. The Church of Ireland had to make a decision as to whether it would indeed be a Protestant sect with carefully delineated edges or whether it would seek in some degree to represent a continuity with the comprehensiveness of the church it had now been at disestablishment. It decided on the latter course but not without struggle and acrimony. The consequence was that the Church of Ireland from that moment onwards feared internal division more than anything else. A phrase in the preface to the *Book of Common Prayer* revised during the 1870s says it all: 'What is imperfect, with peace, is often better than what is otherwise more excellent, without it.' From now on, internal peace would be the *idée fixe* for the Church of Ireland. This explains perhaps better than almost anything else the extraordinary caution that seems to pervade the workings of the Church of Ireland. Certainly there was a move to glorify the centre and to marginalise anything that smacked of extremism, whether the extremism was of a catholic or reformed complexion.

This conviction of the vital necessity for internal unity and harmony, if the Church of Ireland were to survive, has at times come under particular pressure and it continues to do so. The church, perhaps inevitably, has tended to develop in different modes in the years since it occupied two distinct political jurisdictions. There is unquestionably a strong sense of unity but there is also the recognition that difference of opinion and attitude must now be expressed with candour. What I would now wish to say contains generalisations but this is inevitable.

Through the century, the Church of Ireland in the south has numerically become far smaller and a smaller proportion of the population as a whole. That is fact. In addition to a general secularisation, this must be attributed in part to emigration (particularly in the immediate aftermath of the Anglo-Irish war and the civil war) but also to the effects of the draconian Roman Catholic policy on inter-church marriages for most of the century. In consequence, whereas it constitutes a noticeable part of the community in some parts of the Republic, in others it is all but nonexistent. Although it had tended to keep a low profile socially and politically and to live in something of a cultural ghetto (assisted in this by the provision of successive governments to allow the church to have its own educational systems), there are signs of the Church of Ireland in the Republic truly growing in confidence if not in numbers. It has become a recognisable part of the landscape and is perhaps more generally seen as providing a distinctive viewpoint in church matters, and one which may at times deserve to be listened to by the country as a whole. Although no more aligned with the Church of England than before, it has become marginally less insular in attitude and would see its place, in the Anglican family, as in the reformed and catholic tradition.

Inevitably, the Church of Ireland in Northern Ireland has also developed in the context of the culture that surrounds it. Amidst the violence and suspicions of the past thirty years, it has suffered the loss of many of its people, murdered in cold blood for their honest and law-abiding allegiance to a particular political outlook. It is also true that many of its bishops, clergy and people have stood up in the midst of enormous provocation and with remarkable courage in the pursuit of justice, moderation and reconciliation. But it is a community which feels itself under attack and has therefore developed in a very different way from the church in the south. Many members of the church, but by no means all, would regard themselves as primarily within a Protestant rather than an Anglican tradition. The Church of Ireland has the huge advantage that it is a community which within its frontiers contains in Christian fellowship men and women of different national loyalties. But sadly the days when there was a real and constant movement of clergy between north and south seem to have all but gone. Until this present generation, there were very large numbers of southern clergy in Northern Ireland and significant numbers of northern clergy in the Republic. That this is less the case today is to the enormous loss of both communities. A genuine cohesiveness within the Church of Ireland is of great value for this island, north and south. The Church of Ireland in its entirety is the only Christian tradition of any size which does not have a predominantly nationalist or unionist tradition as part of its psyche.

We may be certain that if the churches do not together accept that we can no longer afford the luxury of contending against one another in the context of past shibboleths, prejudices and misconceptions, our days of significance on this island are numbered. The only battle for Christians now is a battle for the credibility of the gospel. The place of the entire Christian Church in the future will not be in the easy complacent centre of things, but out on those margins of belief where so many people in our country now exist, a place between belonging and not belonging to the institutional churches, a place between believing and not believing the faith once delivered to that church. This is a place where the past must be given its perspective, but must never again be our oppressor.

Who are these Irish Presbyterians?

John Dunlop

Back through Scotland to Jerusalem

From some sections of the lovely Antrim Coast Road between Larne and Cushendun, the peninsulas of Scotland appear so close that they seem to be part of Ireland. Across that narrow strip of water the people from the northern part of Ulster and the people of Scotland have travelled back and forth for centuries. At times the Glens of Antrim and the islands of Scotland formed one kingdom.

From the 1600s onwards, people from Scotland came across the water in their thousands, looking for a better way of life and taking advantage of the opportunities which were opened up for them. What was different this time was that the Scottish in-comers were now Presbyterian and were arriving in a place where they were not welcome. Not that it was a religious crusade. The church followed the people.

For an Irish Presbyterian to stand on that road looking across to Scotland, the place from whence we came seems but an arm's length away, while Dundalk, Dublin and Cork can seem a very long way away indeed. The ecclesiological and historical roots of Irish Presbyterians lie across that narrow strip of water and go through Glasgow and Edinburgh to Geneva and thence, through the pre-Reformation church, to Jerusalem, to Jesus and to the apostles, with their definitive affirmations about the significance of Christ.

People of the Word

Ultimate authority within the church lies with Jesus Christ who is regularly, at ordination and installation services of ministers and elders, declared to be 'the sole King and Head of His church'. That authority is exercised through the reading and preaching of the Word of God as it is found in the scriptures of the Old and New Testaments. The reading and preaching of the Word of God, Sunday by Sunday, occupies a very substantial part of a service of worship, sermons seldom lasting less than twenty minutes in a service which lasts a little over an hour, the careful preparation of which occupies a significant part of a minister's weekly responsibilities.

Generally, Presbyterians try to get the language right first and then build the relationships. If they can't agree on the words, then the relationships suffer; even disintegrate. Others may have a different way of approaching this. For them, relationships may come first and words are found which meet the perceived needs of the hour to keep the relationships intact.

There are times when one needs to be precise and accurate, but the demand for too much precision at all times may result in deadlock. Compromise becomes impossible. There are other times when creative flexibility is needed to give people necessary space; but too much of it may cover duplicity and lead ultimately to the total destruction of trust.

The structures of leadership
Leadership within Presbyterian churches is collective rather than individual. The church is distrustful of centralised power. This collective leadership is expressed at every level from the congregation to the General Assembly.

A Moderator of the General Assembly serves for one year only, when he returns from whence he came, lest he gets any notions of being above his station. The Moderator is the principal public representative of the Presbyterian Church for that year, but has no authority to determine church policy.

Women are eligible to be elected to every office in the church, having been eligible for office as ordained elders since 1926 and as ordained ministers since 1976.

Presbyterians are possessed of a conviction that they ought

to be consulted about matters which concern them, having been given the necessary information about any matter about which they are required to take decisions.

Anyone who thinks that people from this tradition are going to be domesticated and turned into easy going people who will agree to nearly anything, doesn't appreciate how the traditions which inform their life have been with them for some hundreds of years. They will not be worn down into a uniformity which destroys their particularity. If they are recognised for what they are and are given space to be true to themselves, they may well co-operate with everyone; but they will not do it if their particularity is discounted.

There are some who say that Presbyterianism is democracy run riot. The church may have influenced the culture of the wider political community as expressed in the Ulster Unionist Party, where the leader is significantly constrained by the necessity of bringing along a vocal and frequently dissenting group of colleagues. The title 'Moderator', rather than 'Leader', might be a better name for that office within that party. This is significantly different from the leadership positions within nationalist and republican parties where the leaders are more like archbishops than moderators.

Finding space or moving on

The Scottish Presbyterians who came to Ireland could not hope to exercise the kind of influence which was exercised by the (Presbyterian) Church of Scotland, so they ran a society within a society, determining their boundaries by doctrinal correctness and internal discipline.[1]

The old Gaelic order having collapsed with the Flight of Earls, the incoming settlers of the plantation, leaving the over populated South West of Scotland, came to a country depopulated by war, but not devoid of inhabitants. Not only were the Presbyterians threatened by the native Irish, they had problems with the established Anglican Church of Ireland and the political authority which underpinned its influence. Presbyterians could only operate schools with permission from the local Church of Ireland bishop; their marriages were not recognised; they could not vote for or sit in the parliament when it was established in College Green, and they had to pay tithes to the Church of Ireland. For the greater part of the eighteenth century Presbyterians were second class citizens in Ulster.

Many Presbyterians left for North America in the 1700s – perhaps as many as 250,000 – where most fought against the British in the American War of Independence. The interaction between those who went to America and those who remained at home helped to lead to the brief alliance between some Presbyterians and Roman Catholics in the 1798 Rebellion.

The 1800s saw the Protestant and Catholic communities growing apart. The Catholic Church was reorganised and reinvigorated under the influence of the ultramontane Cardinal Cullen. A serious schism within the Synod of Ulster in the 1830s led to the creation of what became the Non-Subscribing Presbyterian Church, while the remaining Synod of Ulster united in 1840 with the Secession Synod to form the present General Assembly of the Presbyterian Church in Ireland. A religious revival in 1859 within Protestantism reinvigorated many Protestant, particularly Presbyterian, Churches.

Meanwhile Presbyterians, Methodists and Anglicans coalesced politically within 'unionism' in opposition to 'Home Rule' which they believed would fail to respect the identity and rights of minorities. As a compromise, which was resisted and resented by the Catholic nationalist people of Ireland, Ireland was partitioned.

The scars of the recent troubles
The Presbyterian Church has suffered from very significant shifts of population related directly to the violence of the IRA. There are deep wells of grief within families and congregations who have seen the people they love prematurely laid to rest, often in the quiet churchyards beside the buildings where they worship Sunday by Sunday. The local people have often felt isolated, vulnerable and forgotten by the outside world.

As the possibility of political accommodation is pursued, we must never forget the accumulated legacy of bereavement, injury, dislocation, destruction, anger and mistrust, suffered by people from both parts of the community, which is incalculable. The consequences of violence perpetrated and suffered by both communities will not go away overnight. These matters cannot be simply forgotten, as if nothing has happened.

Presbyterians in Ireland: Fractured and increasingly self-isolating
The Presbyterian Church in Ireland is a member of the World Alliance of Reformed Churches, The Conference of European Churches, The Irish Council of Churches and the Irish Inter Church Meeting. The World Alliance of Reformed Churches provides a link for 161 denominations in 81 countries with 50 million members. There are an additional 10 million Presbyterians not associated with the WARC.

Somewhere in the region of 300,000 people claim connection with the Presbyterian Church in Ireland. It is the largest Protestant church in Northern Ireland and second to the Church of Ireland in the whole island. There are currently 427 ministers in active duty, ministering in 560 congregations, with 65 missionaries serving with churches overseas.

Presbyterians are a fractured community. The various varieties of Presbyterianism in Ireland at present exist in the following approximate numbers in these denominations:

Reformed Presbyterians:	3,400
Free Presbyterians:	13,500
Evangelical Presbyterians:	1,000
Non-Subscribing Presbyterians:	4,500
Presbyterian Church in Ireland:	300,000

It is for me, and many others, a matter of sadness that the Presbyterian Church in Ireland appears to be retreating from its involvement in inter-church and ecumenical activity. The church left the World Council of Churches in 1980; declined to join the Council of Churches of Britain and Ireland, and in June 1999 refused to accept the carefully negotiated proposals which would have brought the Irish Council of Churches and the Irish Inter Church Meeting together to create the Conference of Churches in Ireland.

Oppositional identity

At a conference in 1998 at Notre Dame University in Illinois on the theme of 'The Sacred, the Sword and Global Security', Dr Marc Gopin,[2] from the Centre for Strategic and International Studies in Washington DC, spoke from within the Jewish Community of how threatened communities seek to consolidate their identities and use their traditions to that end, overlooking the resources within their traditions for conflict resolution. They look for marks which distinguish them from others.

One can see manifestations of this within Presbyterianism, as threatened people look for theological formulations to bolster self-identity and overlook the shared material which could bring people closer together, without losing their individuality.

That which energises some people, in both religious and political communities, and the glue which holds them together within their separate groups, has a large negative element to it. In the Catholic nationalist community a significant element of the negative energy comes from anti-Britishness; in the Protestant unionist community from anti-Catholicism.

It is noteworthy that it is only recently that people in the Republic of Ireland have begun to emerge out of the shadow of Britain to a more honoured, secure and equal place with others within the European Union, thereby gaining a more confident sense of selfworth.

Oppositional identity operates within communities as well as between them. The Protestant/unionist community is deeply fractured into many varieties of Protestantism and many varieties of unionism; each of them much given to a rehearsal of difference and a downplaying of common ground. There is a cohesiveness about the Catholic/nationalist community which is not replicated in the other section of the community.

Self-determination or secure belonging for minorities and majorities?

Dr Duncan Morrow, from the Faculty of Humanities in the University of Ulster, put it at a recent conference[3] at New College in the University of Edinburgh:

> After World War I the notion of self-determination was developed as a defence against autocratic power, but the concept of self-determination can now be used in the service of the massive suppression of minorities. Self-determination can be seen as right exercised over against other people. History as 'righteous cause' traps some people inside the gates and traps others outside as 'unrighteous'.

The Good Friday Agreement modifies this notion of self-determination.

The trouble with nationalism and unionism, and the kind of republicanism with which we have become familiar, is that they provide some people with a sense of belonging while excluding others. Only some are embraced. Neither ideology has managed to enhance the quality of self-esteem of people in both parts of the community.

Is complex British/Irish identity politically permissible? Professor Terence Brown,[4] of Trinity College Dublin, put the matter well when he wrote:

> The nationalist mind-set customarily finds the idea of an Irish person readily identifying himself or herself as British an evident absurdity.

Many Irish Presbyterians in Northern Ireland find the notion of being both British and Irish very attractive. Presbyterians who have lived in what is now the Republic of Ireland, whose numbers have greatly reduced since partition, have now abandoned all sense of being British. Perhaps it was the price that had to be paid to be accepted in the new Irish State.

We need to affirm that everyone, regardless of ethnicity or race, is made in the image of God and therefore significant and valuable. The rights which people have are founded on the fact that they are made in the image of God, a reality of prior significance to religious affiliation, race, gender or political allegiance.

Mourning for loss

The trend whereby Presbyterians, as well as Anglicans and Methodists, no longer try to buy houses in many parts of Belfast is a tragic manifestation of demographic suicide, leaving schools and churches marooned. In the imagery of Isaiah chapter 1, 'The daughter of Zion is left like a cottage in a vineyard, like a lodge in a garden of cucumbers ...' after the activity of harvest is over. These schools and church buildings speak of what once was, but is no more.

Such have been the shifts of population in Northern Ireland that it is estimated that out of a population of 1.5 million, less than 100,000 now live in integrated areas where the population mix is within 10 per cent of 50 per cent. Even within these areas there are exclusive enclaves. Such is the legacy of thirty years of terrorism. We are describing a demographic disaster, which spans social classes. Shifts in population have led to the creation of homogeneous areas where the experience of living together with people of the 'other' community is now limited. As a consequence, it is difficult to sustain church and community life in an area where the number of people in what was a previously mixed community has fallen.

Declining Protestant populations are particularly evident around the border. In my own home town of Newry, a town just north of the border, the Protestant population has fallen consistently over the last thirty years of violence. My home Presbyterian congregation is half the size of what it was when I was growing up in the town. There were two viable 'Protestant' primary schools in my school days. My old school is now closed. Where it was once possible to organise enthusiastic youth work with significant numbers of young people, this is no longer possible. One Presbyterian friend said to me the other day, in a mood of deep depression, that in her town 'We no longer matter'. A community in decline can suffer acute depression when its community life ceases to be viable. Its story needs to be heard.

Majorities often fail to recognise what they do to other people. Hardly anyone in Ireland does not belong to some majority or other. Majorities in any town or locality or country need to look out for and look after their minorities; asking of them how they are and how they feel and then listening to the answers.

The present state of hopefulness

The report of the Church and Government Committee to the 1999 General Assembly[5] contained the following:

A place where we can all feel at home

The majority support given to the 'Good Friday Agreement' by people in Northern Ireland and in the Republic of Ireland in concurrent referenda, along with the subsequent elections and meetings of the new Northern Ireland Assembly, give rise to optimism that we have entered a new era of peaceful political co-operation within and between the people of these islands. We are a damaged and suspicious political community which has been through very difficult times and it will take time to heal these wounds. It remains a priority that trust be built between the different parts of our community and between elected representatives of the people so that co-operation becomes a reality.

The ideologies of Ulster unionism and Irish nationalism failed to provide everyone with a sense of belonging, while militant republicanism and militant loyalism visited untold damage on thousands of people. The opportunity now exists for us to get beyond these exclusive and excluding ideologies to arrangements which will provide us all with a sense of being accepted and honoured. Both parts of this island ought to be places where people from different backgrounds feel at home; where we provide each other with a sense of belonging; where no-one feels like a stranger and where responsibilities and opportunities are shared.

The inward focus of legitimate pastoral concern which has tended to bind churches to their communities, illustrates how easy it is for churches to find themselves shackled to communities which are in conflict with one another. It is easy to understand how churches become trapped within the anxieties, the prejudices and the convictions of the wider communities from which ministers, priests, elders and members are drawn and of which they are a continuing part.

The Croatian theologian Miroslav Volf[6] maintained that it is clear what we should turn away from. 'It is captivity to our own culture, coupled so often with blind self-righteousness.' But, he asks:

> What should we turn to? ... What should be the relation of the churches to the cultures they inhabit? The answer lies ... in cultivating the proper relation between distance from the culture and belonging to it ... The proper distance from a culture does not take a Christian out of that culture. Christians are not the insiders who have taken flight to a new 'Christian culture' and become outsiders to their own culture; rather when they have responded to the call of the gospel they have stepped, as it were, with one foot outside their own culture while with the other remaining firmly planted in it. They are distant and yet they belong. Their difference is internal to the culture.

Volf explored the concept of 'double embrace',[7] based on the parable of the loving father in Luke 15. The father refused to have his identity defined in an exclusive relationship with either one of his two sons. The father did not allow himself to be trapped in acceptance of one son and rejection of the other. He loved the older boy a good deal more than most preachers manage to do. The father refused to succumb to the philosophy of the elder brother's strategy of 'it's either him or me'. For the father, it was both at the same time.

In conformity with the grace of God, can churches in Ireland escape from entrapment in single embraces and model a different way of proceeding?

Let us imagine that God has two children in Ireland; one Catholic/nationalist; the other Protestant/unionist. Is it possible for us to speak about God as the Father who is the parent to both of these two children; we, whoever we are, being one of them?

If this is the case, then in conformity with the grace of God,

can we in our churches escape from entrapment in single embraces and model a different way of proceeding as we journey
from one millennium to another?

Notes:

1. *Authority in the Church,* edited by Seán Mac Réamoinn, The Columba
Press, 1995. Chapter on 'Authority in the Presbyterian Church' by
Terence McCaughey, p 90.
2. Gopin Marc, Paper on: 'Constructing Paradigms of Religious Conflict
in a Modern Context: A Case Study of Judaism'. The paper will form a
chapter in a book to be published next year by the Oxford University
Press under the title *Between Eden and Armageddon: The Future of World
Religions, Violence, Peacemaking.*
3. 'A Turning Point in Ireland and Scotland? The Challenge to the
Churches and Theology', The Centre for Theology and Public Issues,
New College, The University of Edinburgh, 27/28 February 1998.
4. Brown, Terence, 'British Ireland' in *Culture in Ireland – Division or
Diversity?,* edited by Edna Longley, Institute of Irish Studies, Queen's
University Belfast, 1991, p 74.
5. General Assembly, Annual Reports, 1999, p 16.
6. Volf, Miroslav, *Exclusion and Embrace,* Abingdon, 1996, p 37.
7. Volf, op. cit., p 156.

Minorities Cherished and Affirmed

Robert Dunlop

Back in the fifties a member of our congregation attended a rural National School in the neighbourhood. One day her teacher announced that the Church of Ireland was the biggest church in America! Neither the wild inaccuracy nor the grotesque bias of this claim troubled her too much at the time. But internally she felt humiliated and isolated on hearing the news from an authority figure that the minority denomination to which she belonged locally was inconsequential everywhere. Statistically, the facts were turned on their head – the Episcopal Church, USA is actually one of the smaller denominations while the Baptists are the largest Protestant body in the United States.

The teacher had failed to do her homework and the slip showed. This anecdote raises the important question of minorities – their status, their significance and their sensibilities.

Minorities – a mixed bag

Belonging to a religious minority is something of a mixed blessing – on the one hand it facilitates a feeling of distinctiveness, but, on the other, it presents the perilous possibility of sliding into isolationism. Sometimes 'small is beautiful' but frequently 'small is burdensome'. As the social and religious climate in Ireland undergoes a hasty metamorphosis, it is anticipated that intolerance of smaller entities will begin to wane.

Ian Linden has argued that 'part of any post-modern spirituality has to be an acknowledgement of the Other in all their difference'. He sees this recognition as a key development lying 'at the heart of any successful building of coalitions for change in which religious and Christian groups may participate'. (*Doctrine and Life*, July/August, 1999)

We are still grappling with the challenge of coming to terms with a world 'incorrigibly plural' and, in Louis MacNeice's appropriate phrase, wondering what it is like to 'feel the drunkenness of things being various'. Such a spectacle, it might be said, demands sober reflection!

Being positively various

The Christian churches, especially those who have enjoyed majority status, would do well to begin by taking into their purview their own sub-divisions.

Minorities have a long and distinguished provenance, especially those spawned out of deep conviction and at personal cost. They came into being for a variety of reasons, some noble and reasonable, others ignoble and questionable. Communities were sometimes gathered as a form of protest against the excesses, inconsistencies and crass worldliness of the *status quo* versions of the faith. They often emerged with cathartic intent as well as revisionist zeal. In assessing their significance and coming to terms with their ethos, it is essential to be accurately informed about their originating purpose as well as their subsequent focus. From the perspective of viewing the big picture and asking where do the smaller editions fit in, nothing is lost and much is gained by getting hold of as many factual details as possible.

A global perspective

Christianity is now heralded as a world faith with over two billion adherents. While it is declining rapidly in European countries, there is impressive numerical growth in Africa and Asia. A struggling minority in Europe may be a numerous, vibrant and influential body somewhere else. There are some statistical surprises when the situation is surveyed globally. One study has yielded the interesting figures in the table opposite.

Denomination	Community	% of population
Anglican	53,200,000	1%
Baptist	67,100,000	1%
Roman Catholic	912,600,000	16%
Indigenous	35,200,000	0.5%
Lutheran	84,500,000	2%
Methodist	25,600,000	0.5%
Orthodox	139,500,000	2%
Pentecostal	105,800,000	2%
Presbyterian	48,000,000	1%
Other Churches	142,500,000	2%

(*They call themselves Christian*, Christian Research and The Lausanne Committee for World Evangelization, 1999, page 82.)

This breakdown, while far from exhaustive, discloses that denominations which are a tiny minority in one part of the world may represent something quite different in another country. It gives the sort of global perspective which enables majority bodies to evaluate their size in worldwide as against purely local terms, and facilitates minorities in seeing themselves against a backdrop which reaches beyond the parochial and immediate.

Towards a working definition
By definition, a minority may be described in the following terms:

'A group numerically inferior to the rest of the population of a state, in a non-dominant position, whose members – being nationals of the state – possess ethnic, religious or linguistic characteristics differing from those of the rest of the population and show, if only implicitly, a sense of solidarity, directed towards preserving their culture, traditions, religion or language.' (*United Nations Declaration*)

In Ireland, the pilgrimage towards pluralism opens the way for frank discourse on the place of minorities in our changing society. At this stage in the journey, it is possible to identify some discernible trends. With the break-up of the old absolutist mono-culture, we are being forced to cast an enquiring eye on the otherness of the other. Generally speaking, the climate of the times encourages some sort of respect for difference, diversity and even dissent. On the ground, the symbiotic identity of both the Catholic/nationalist and the Protestant/unionist equations has fallen under the investigative spotlight. This has resulted in the freeing up of the perceptive process through which diverseness isn't looked upon as perverseness. The unlocking of the cultural impasse and the collapse of monolithic assumptions enable us to identify the undergrowth needing to be removed as we edge towards toleration and accommodation.

Making space for minorities

The millennium offers a fitting opportunity for stocktaking and serious re-evaluation, especially on the part of dominant majorities. A position of privilege inevitably carries a price tag and demands a stringent interior audit. Theologically, the insights of Reinhold Niebuhr throw up such a challenge:

> 'A democratic society must use every stratagem of education and every resource of religion to generate appreciation of the virtues and good intentions of minority groups which diverge from the type of the majority, and to prompt humility and charity in the life of the majority.'

Pronouncements on behalf of the four main churches, while often well crafted and well intentioned, tend to give the impression of ubiquitous collegiality and church consensus, *una voce*. When this happens, minority opinion is easily smothered, ignored or sidelined. The comments of the Quakers, the Congregationalists, the Baptists, the Covenanters, the Pentecostals, the Unitarians, the Moravians, the Salvation Army, the Christian (Plymouth) Brethren, the Seventh Day Adventists, are seldom sought or offered in the arena of public discourse.

While small faith communities may be shy to speak out, this doesn't mean they have nothing to say. If their opinions remain unsought they may well retreat into silence. Part of the responsibility of larger bodies is to create space for the convictions, insights and opinions of minorities to find expression. It is not enough to defend their right to exist. They need and deserve a lot more than what happened all too often in the past – a patronising concession which set out to protect their right to be wrong!

At best, smaller communities are well positioned to survey the scene from the edge. They have the potential to contribute clarity of vision and the sort of prophetic voice which rises out of being disencumbered with ecclesiastical protocol. It is not unknown for the edge to become the cutting edge. If they are to function in any meaningful way they must be given room to articulate their convictions and concerns and, where necessary, to air their grievances. Furthermore, those who have inherited numerical strength or widespread influence should be the first to assume the mantle of guardianship, acting as guarantors of the value and voice of smaller entities. The Uppsala Statement of the World Council of Churches in 1968 presses home the point:

'Most nations have ethnic, cultural or religious minorities. These minorities have the right to choose for themselves their own way of life insofar as this choice does not deny the same choice to other groups. Majorities can be insensitive and tyrannical, and minorities may need protection. This is a special responsibility for the church of Him who is the champion of the oppressed ... But if pressed too far, the rights of minorities can destroy justice and threaten the stability or the existence of the nation. The frustration of a majority by a minority is as incompatible with justice as the persecution of a minority by a majority.'

A wide spectrum and multiple voices

It must be recognised that religious minorities represent quite a wide spectrum and include both negative and positive characteristics. The causes and circumstances of their formation determine their overall *raison d'être*, posture and stance on interests and issues. Their own self definition may differ significantly from the external perception on the part of those who observe them. It is incumbent upon larger communities to gather knowledge of the originating focus of the minority group. Frequently, smaller religious denominations seceded from a more numerous body, often resulting in both distancing and disowning.

Religious sub-divisions display diverse origins and emphases. It is helpful to think in terms of four distinct manifestations:

1. Churches in the Christian tradition who have detached themselves from the dominant established (state) church but who remain in touch with the historical communities.

2. Christian denominations and congregations which have separated from the wider ecclesial bodies and live independently or as separatist groups.

3. Groups whose approach to faith and whose doctrines and practices are alien to the biblical tradition, including esoteric, spiritualist cults.

4. Syncretistic formations where the non-Christian element predominates , like Christian Scientists.

In the Reformation and post-Reformation era many new faith communities were formed, some remaining as minorities, others such as the Baptists and Presbyterians, gathering large followings. Included in these dissenters or nonconformists are Waldensians, Moravians, Congregationalists, Quakers and Baptists. Methodists arose in the eighteenth century in a time of religious revival and became a major force in Evangelical Christianity. They retained a recognition of their Anglican roots. While they developed into a separate denomination in the eighteenth century, the umbilical cord attaching them to the parent body has never been totally severed.

Whether looking at sub-divisions within the stream of Christian orthodoxy or the more radical groupings, it is important to engage with the thought processes of a minority community. Almost without exception they came into being because of a desire to rediscover or maintain some forgotten doctrine or insight within the overall framework of Christian revelation. This inevitably produced treasured distinctives which occupy a permanent place within the crop of core convictions.

Sometime these central emphases are obvious – most people know that Quakers stress the idea of 'inner light', Methodists are 'methodical', Mennonites are 'peaceable', Pentecostals are strong on 'living in the Spirit', Congregationalists make much of the 'gathered church', Baptists practice 'believers' immersion'. In no way do these descriptions disclose all that needs to be known about any of these bodies. Therefore, if they are to be taken seriously they need to be asked to speak for themselves, to clarify what they believe and how they function. For this to happen there needs to be a tuning-in process so that the wider entities get on to their wavelength and avoid distortion. Such a friendly investigation should be prompted by more than suspicion or curiosity. If it is sustained as part of a learning curve, the outcome will be informative and positive.

Unfencing the narrow ground

It is all too easy for smaller communities to be treated as substandard, eccentric or just a bothersome nuisance! As long as they are regarded as insignificant mavericks, they will struggle in an atmosphere of religious opprobrium and/or be dismissed as dispensable pariahs.

Most minorities have either stated or felt fears. Three of the most common are domination, distortion and assimilation. Often they cling to the narrow ground because they are assigned no wider space by those who think they have divine rights to the whole field. The rest are really only squatters, who, when they reach maturity will either die out or move on and leave the Big Country to the ecclesiastical ranchers who are driven by the 'winner takes all' policy. The consequences of this distancing of dissent penetrate both those who represent the majority identity and those who are in a minor place. When distinctiveness is ignored, damage ensues.

The pain of distortion is hard to bear, especially when sweeping generalisations are made, with little or no attempt to define and describe precisely or even accurately. For example, it is not unusual for churches who belong to the Evangelical tradition to be labelled or dismissed as 'fundamentalists'. When the term is used in a pejorative way, as is often the case, serious misrepresentation takes place. 'Non-recognition or misrecognition can inflict harm, can be a form of oppression, imprisoning someone in a false, distorted and reduced mode of being.' (Charles Taylor)

Turning the argument around, it is vitally important to spell out the responsibilities of minorities in their relationship with the larger entities. If they do not enjoy the sort of self-worth which gives credibility to their existence they will inevitably go down the defensive road and venture out only to fire salvos at the ruling opposition. This inner emigration gnaws into the vitals of their being. At worst, it contorts them into an isolated and even a destructive element. Sadly, their creativity is in danger of being killed at source simply because they lack the oxygen of the market place. Paradoxically, they will be tempted to ape the majority in order to raise their own profile

When religious minorities open themselves to the big picture and embrace an authentic inclusivism, they are actually contributing to their own affirmation and enrichment. Numerical strength should not be confused with either efficiency or spiritual credibility. When the little people become debunkered, their voice may well be caught by the fair wind to become a clarion call. We only have to think of the courageous and pervasive impact of the Italian Waldensians, 'older than Luther and smaller than the Scottish Episcopalians'. In Ireland, the contribution of the Quakers to both civil and religious society is well documented and widely agreed. The Mennonites number less than a million worldwide but as a Peace Church they have made a major contribution to peacemaking and conflict resolution.

When minorities are given a *niche* on which to take their stand they really come into their own as their cup overflows. They too are subject to the crippling advances of consumerism and secularisation which so pointedly afflict the larger bodies. Unless they engage in a regular interior review and assess their distinctive contribution to the wider world, they can easily fade into non-existence. How sad that only a few hundred Samaritans remain at Mt Gerizim and the famed Shakers in New England are reduced to a handful. What a pity that the only remaining Moravian 'presence' in Dublin is a burial ground, and the last Congregational church in the city at Kilmainham is struggling to keep going.

The third Millenium is likely to produce a fresh crop of religious dissenters now that the old monopolies of the nineteenth century are broken and it is no longer socially alien to belong to a worshipping body outside the pale. Many Free Church communities share some of the theological and ecclesiological convictions of the historic minorities such as the Anabaptists, the Congregationalists and the Moravians. They may be still finding their feet, but they are here to stay. They may well become the fresh voice, so much part of the nonconformist confessions in the past four hundred years. There is an engaging irony in President Madison's famous quip that American religious harmony was based on a multiplicity of sects, all of whom disagreed with each other! On this side of the Atlantic, we are still more culture bound spiritually and socially.

Yet healthy diversity may well create a sharper vision of the future. Ireland is going to need all the spiritual muscle it can muster if the tide of secularism is to be confronted. What counts ultimately is not size but authenticity. For this reason, minorities matter. They deserve to be cherished and affirmed.

There is more than a little mileage in the wise and prophetic words of Teresa of Avila: 'Nothing is small if God accepts it.'

The Jewish Contribution
to twentieth-century Ireland

Dermot Keogh

Numerical decline

'The smaller we get, the stronger we get', was how Alex Jaffe from Belfast saw, at the end of the 1980s, the future of a community in rapid decline.[1] That was trying to put a good face on a bad situation. But the remark was not untypical of what one might have heard in the 1990s south of the border in Dublin where a rapidly declining community took the momentous decision in 1999 to sell the beautiful 100-year-old synagogue at Adelaide Road. The main and more modern synagogue in Belfast had been divided in two to cater for an ever-decreasing congregation.

The post-World War II years had provided many difficult challenges for the Jewish Congregation in Ireland. South of the border, the decline was steady but not quite as acute as in Northern Ireland. In 1946, the total Jewish population on the island was 5,381 (3,907 in the Republic of Ireland and 1,474 in Northern Ireland). By 1961, the community had been reduced to 4,446 for the island (3,255 in the Republic and 1,191 in the North).[2] The figures for Northern Ireland dropped steadily from 959 in 1971 to 517 in 1981. It was down to 410 in 1991, and most members of that community were over fifty.[3] The drop in the Republic of Ireland was from 2,633 in 1971 to 2,127 in 1981 and to 1,580 in 1991. By the mid-1990s the number was between 1,000 and 1,200.[4]

The demographic decline may be illustrated more clearly by focusing on the smaller towns. There were 252 Jews living in Cork city and county in 1946; that figure has dropped from 120 in 1961 to 62 in 1981. In Waterford city and county there were no Jews returned as living there in 1981; the drop had been from 23 in 1946 to 4 in 1971.

Dublin, the capital of the Republic, remained the most important centre of Jewish life. Writing in 1987, the historical geographer, Dr Stanley Waterman, described the process of decline thus:

Today, when one speaks of the Jewish community in Ireland, the reference is almost exclusively to Dublin. Over most of the past hundred years, Dublin has consistently accounted for 80 per cent of the Jews living in the twenty-six counties that constitute the Republic of Ireland, and, since 1936, over 90 per cent ... Earlier in the century, Limerick and Waterford too had small congregations. However, today, Belfast has dwindled to little over 300 persons and the Cork community is, to all intents and purposes, defunct.[5]

According to a study by J. J. Sexton and R. O'Leary, the annual average rate of decline was 1.2 per cent in the period from 1946 to 1961. That rose to nearly 3 per cent in the intercensal 1981-91 period.[6] The ageing of the Jewish population was another indicator of decline. Only 3 per cent of the population was over 65 years in 1926, compared with a quarter in 1991. According to the same study, about 9 per cent of the Jewish population were aged under five in 1926 compared with 4.5 per cent in 1991. Some 25 per cent of the population were over 65 according to the 1991 census, compared with 3.3 per cent in 1926 and 4.5 per cent in 1936. That figure rose to 6.7 per cent in 1946, 10.6 per cent in 1961 and 21.4 per cent in 1981.[7]

However, the main reason for the drop in the numbers of the community was emigration to Britain, the United States of America, Canada and Israel.

The decline, according to Dr Waterman, was more significant than a mere loss of numbers:

It wasn't just a numerical decline at that time, but something much more subtle, a metamorphosis of an immigrant community. For, during the fifty or sixty years or so that the modern community had been in existence, specific individuals or families had made specific community institutions their own personal fief. When they left the scene, the removal of what had often been a forceful personality with a lifelong involvement led to a qualitative decline too.'[8]

The community had moved on since the 1950s when the Chief Rabbi, Immanuel Jakobovits, wrote about the Jewish communities in Ireland being modelled broadly on the Anglo-Jewish pattern subject to four modifying factors. Firstly, Ireland had been one of the few European countries not directly involved in World War II. Secondly, unlike the other two neutral states in Europe (Sweden and Switzerland), Ireland had hardly any influx of refugees before, during, or after the war. The result was that Jewish life thus tended to be very conservative, as it remained uninfluenced by continental newcomers. (Over 80 per cent of the Jewish households in the country used kosher meat.)[9] Thirdly, the ratio of Jews to the rest of the population was very low, perhaps the smallest in any English-speaking country. Fourthly, Jakobovits observed that Irish Jews live in a staunchly Catholic environment – about 93 per cent of the population belong to the Roman Catholic Church. As a consequence of those factors, he concluded that Jewish life was marked by a relatively great degree of social isolation and self-containment.[10]

Jakobovits profiled the local Jewish community as leading a separate existence from that of British Jewry. This was accentuated since the passage in 1949 of the External Relations Act which had taken Ireland out of the Commonwealth.[11] Links between the communities in Belfast and Dublin were quite strong up to the late 1960s. Marriage between members of the two communities was quite common. Tennis tournaments, sporting and cultural events were organised. Social contact, however, between Dublin and Belfast was significantly curtailed following the outbreak of conflict in Northern Ireland in the late 1960s which has, with a short respite of two years, continued into the late 1990s.[12]

Belfast
Belfast, like Dublin, also witnessed the relocation of its Jewish community. In 1926 a Jewish Institute had been built in Ashfield

Gardens, off Glandore Avenue. This two-storey building had a restaurant and tennis courts. It was the home of the Jewish Dramatic Society and the Junior Forum debating society. In the 1930s and 1940s some families continued to move out to the edge of the suburbs along the Antrim Road, Donegall Park Avenue and Waterloo Road. By the 1950s there was an estimated 25% of the Belfast community in the Malone area. An attempt to open a synagogue in the area was discouraged by Rabbi Schacter. However, by the end of the 1950s and early 1960s many members of the community lived in the upper part of the Antrim Road, i.e. Waterloo Park, Donegall Park Avenue and the Shaftesbury area near Belfast Castle. That was too far for the older members of the community to walk to the synagogue in Carlisle Circus. The President of the community, Barnie Hurwitz, raised over £80,000 in the early 1960s to build a new synagogue and community centre in Somerton Road, which was opened in 1964 and could seat 1,500. But the dwindling community in the 1980s and 1990s necessitated the dividing of the main synagogue and the selling off of some of the adjacent buildings.[13]

Dublin

Historically, the Jewish community in Dublin had been concentrated on both sides of the river in the inner city area. Over twenty per cent of Jewish households in 1941 were concentrated in a single 25-hectare grid in the South Circular Road area.[14] The more prosperous members of the community had moved to Rathmines, Blackrock or Dún Laoghaire. A number also lived in the Ballsbridge area. There was also a significant shift in the Jewish population to an area between Harold's Cross and Terenure in the south. There was also a move to the area from Rathmines to Rathgar.[15] The Jewish community since the 1930s had been moving from 'Little Jerusalem' in the South Circular Road area, southwards to Rathmines. As orthodox Jews walk to and from synagogue, it was decided to establish the Rathmines Hebrew Congregation in the mid-1930s. Services were held in the homes of B. Citron of Grosvenor Road and L. Epstein of Grosvenor Place. The Church of Ireland parochial hall on

Leinster Rd was made available to the community to conduct service on High Holy Day. A permanent synagogue was later acquired on Grosvenor Rd. But as many members of the congregation were young couples with families now living in the nearby suburb of Terenure, a site was purchased there by the members of the Grosvenor congregation. While funds were being raised for a new synagogue, services on the site were first conducted in a Nissen hut. The Terenure Hebrew Congregation Synagogue opened in 1953. An arson attack in the mid-1960s did considerable damage to the building. Local Catholic and Protestant clergy offered their halls for the use of religious service. The synagogue was re-opened in 1966.

Terenure, with its new synagogue, thus replaced South Circular Road as the most important residential area for Dublin Jews. The synagogues were served by the Chief Rabbi and by Dayan Z. Alony.[16] By the 1980s, the seven *chevras* (conventicles) in the south Circular Road had disappeared. The Walworth Road Synagogue had been converted into a Jewish museum which was opened by the President of Israel, Chaim Herzog, while on an official visit to Dublin in 1985.[17]

What remains of that once throbbing artery of Jewish life around the South Circular Road, asks Asher Benson ruefully: 'the Adelaide Road synagogue, the Jewish Museum, a few Jewish-owned homes, two kosher butcher shops in Clanbrassil Street and one kosher bakery in Lennox Street owned by a non-Jew'.[18] Dublin had, by the 1960s, lost its 'Little Jerusalem'. By the end of the twentieth century, Ireland had a rapidly declining Jewish community.

The Irish state and anti-semitism in the 1950s

Upward social mobility partially explains the reason for the opening of a Jewish golf club at Edmondstown.[19] But the reason for this was also related to the prevalence of an anti-Jewish bias detected by members of the community who had been refused membership in other clubs for no good reason. The Jewish community in Belfast opened their own section in Fortwilliam golf club after similar experiences of discrimination.

How did Rabbi Jakobovits view the relationship between Jews and the Irish state in the post-war period?

In so far as these relations are exemplified by the treatment of the small Jewish community in Ireland, they are certainly close and cordial. The rights of Jewish citizens as equals among the other denominational groups are expressly recognised in a special clause of the Irish constitution – probably the only Jewish community in the world to be constitutionally protected in this explicit manner. In practice, too, the Jews of Ireland have always felt free from discrimination. In fact, Ireland is one of the very few countries that has never blemished its record by any serious anti-Jewish outrages.[20]

Yet, anti-semitism remained a peripheral sub-current in Irish society in the 1950s. The decision to set up a Jewish golf club was not, as has been mentioned, exclusively or indeed primarily motivated by the affluence associated with upward social mobility. There continued to be significant discrimination among the middle classes against Jews in Dublin in the 1950s. The US envoy Chapin reported in 1949 that, although anti-Semitic feeling had not been common in Ireland, some prejudice had arisen around that time as a result of the fact that Jews 'are accumulating real estate and monopolies to a noticeable degree'. He claimed that Jews had purchased property so extensively in the once-fashionable Dublin summer resort of Bray that the town was 'now termed "Little Palestine"'.[21] While Chapin's remarks were hardly rooted in serious sociological research, he was most probably recycling a prejudice fashionable in his Dublin milieu.

While Jewish leaders in Dublin could do little to combat such attitudes, they had little alternative but to confront the ideas put forward by the members of *Maria Duce* (Under the leadership of Mary), a society founded in 1945 by Fr Denis Fahey. Its literature represented in tone and content the continuation of interwar anti-Jewish propaganda. It wrote about alleged Judeo-Masonic control of the United States, the United Nations, the international press and cinema, and transnational business.[22] Its newspaper, *Fiat*, also attacked the Irish Association for Civil

Liberties which was presided over by Seán Ó Faoláin. The painter, Louis Le Brocquy, was also a member as was Senator Owen Sheehy Skeffington.[23] According to the gardaí, elements from *Maria Duce* were responsible for the publication of an anti-semitic sheet, *Saoirse* (Freedom) which appeared on 9 September 1950. The secretary of the Jewish Representative Council, Ernest Newman, called on the Taoiseach, John A. Costello, on 30 October 1950 accompanied by his father, Arthur. Costello sent them to the Department of Justice where they saw two senior officials, Peter Berry and Dan Costigan. The latter told them that the government was most anxious to avoid 'any racial trouble in this country and that they could be expected to take any action within their power to prevent any encouragement of racial prejudice'.

After investigation, it was discovered that the *Saoirse* news sheet had a negligible circulation. Published at irregular intervals, it was distributed outside the General Post Office in Dublin. A minute in the Department of Justice recorded: 'While it is anti-Jewish, it is mild in tone compared with a previous anti-Jewish publication called 'Penapa'.'[24] Its contents were not deemed to be subversive nor did any of the articles amount to criminal libel. The issue of *Saoirse* in the archives carries the headline: 'Communism is Jewish'.[25] The gardaí knew the man responsible for its publication and that it came from the offices of Aontas Náisiúnta in Pearse St. The general advice from the gardaí to the Jewish community was to 'ignore the existence of this periodical'.[26] The IRA raided the *Saoirse* premises on 23 September 1950. No further issues of the paper appeared to trouble the leaders of the Jewish community.[27] As for *Maria Duce*, it never attracted mass support and it declined steadily in influence during the latter part of the 1950s only, finally, to disappear in the 1960s.[28] There may have been incidents of general unpleasantness in the 1950s involving religious minorities in Ireland. But it differed radically in tone from the temper of the 1930s.[29]

Involvement in politics

Despite the need to defend their community, Jews in the 1950s –
or since the foundation of the state – did not show a willingness
to play an active role in national politics. Jakobovits noted that,
while 'Irish Jews suffer no civic or political disabilities, few are
to be found in politics or the civil service.'[30] At that time, Fianna
Fáil's Robert Briscoe was the exception. (Herman Good had
been an unsuccessful candidate for the Labour Party in the 1944
election.) A TD since 1927, it was a source of great pride in the
community when, in 1956, Briscoe was elected Lord Mayor of
Dublin. Rabbi Jakobovits delivered a sermon on 8 July at
Greenville hall synagogue:

> By his election, he has not only raised himself to a stature of
> world repute, to be the most prominent Jew ever born within
> these shores. He has also uplifted our standing, and turned
> the attention and regard of Jewish communities throughout
> the world to Irish Jewry. Not since my illustrious predecessor
> was called from Dublin to assume the highest spiritual office
> in Jewry as Chief Rabbi of the Holy Land, has our community
> featured so conspicuously in the Jewish press in Israel, in the
> United States, in England, and in virtually every other land
> of our dispersion.[31]

Briscoe, who served in Dáil Éireann until 1965, was again
elected Lord Mayor in 1961/62.[32] A small number of a later generation of Jews, in the 1970s and 1980s, would choose politics as
a profession.

The Jewish Community honours de Valera

The Jewish community in Ireland, despite its justifiable concern
about manifestations of anti-semitism, have had occasion to single out one politician, Éamon de Valera, as worthy of singular
mention for his work on behalf religious minorities. In particular, the leaders of that community had been aware throughout
the 1930s and 1940s of the work he had done on behalf of Jews.
De Valera retired from party political life in 1959 and became
President the same year. He held that position until 1973.[33]

In recognition of de Valera's contribution to public life, the Irish Jewish community decided to honour him in 1963. It was proposed to plant a forest of 10,000 trees in Israel named after the Irish President in recognition of his many years of devoted service in the cause of peace and freedom. The site chosen for the forest was Kfar Kanna, near Nazareth. All relevant matters regarding the proposed forest were administered by the Éamon de Valera Forest Committee under the chairmanship of Mervyn L. Abrahamson.[34]

The ceremonial planting of the first tree took place on 18 August 1966.[35] The Israeli Prime Minister, Levi Eshkol, in a letter to Abrahamson for the occasion, said: 'I see in the planting of trees in President de Valera's distinguished name a fitting expression of the traditional friendship between the Irish and the Jewish peoples, two nations that have so much in common of history and fulfilment.'[36] Eshkol hoped that the forest would serve in its green growth to strengthen and multiply the links of mutual regard and respect between Ireland and Israel.[37]

Jacob Herzog, the Political Director in Eshkol's office, also wrote to Abrahamson on 18 August. While the tone of the letter is appropriately celebratory, the text also contains evidence of the close relationship which continued to exist between de Valera and the Herzog family after the Chief Rabbi's departure for Palestine in 1937:

> The name of Éamon de Valera is not only enshrined for all time on the tablets of Irish independence. His name is a byword across the world as one of the pioneers of the present epoch in human history, a central theme of which is the emergence of small countries to independence, their assertion of their freedom and right to pursue their national destiny without external interference and to make their contribution on the international scene in equality.[38]

Radio Israel covered the ceremony and the commentary was given by the former actor and Irish civil servant, Cork-born Lawrence Elyan who had emigrated from Ireland some years before. The prayer recited at the ceremony was as follows:

In the forest in honour of
Eamon de Valera
Make deep their roots and wide their crown
Amongst all the trees of Israel,
For good for beauty.

The Irish-born Israeli diplomat, Max Nurock, spoke at the ceremony. He said of De Valera:

Among the countless public rewards and recognitions that he has merited by outstanding quality and performance as mathematician, soldier and statesman, indeed as one of the world's great minds, penetrating, compassionate and res-olute, that distinguished Irishman has richly earned today's tribute in Israel by showing himself to be a constant and stal-wart wellwisher of Jewry and of the Jewish State.[39]

The *Jewish Chronicle* reported that de Valera was 'thrilled' at the honour that had been accorded him by the dedication of the de Valera Forest at Kfar Kana.[40]

De Valera's closeness with the Herzog family in particular was later revealed in a letter from the widow of Jacob Herzog, P'nina, on 20 April 1972 following the death of her husband:

It is still only a few desolate weeks since Jacob died, and the anguish of my inexpressible loss is deep and enduring. But I find comfort in proud retrospect upon his life and works, and upon his manifold friendships. In those healing memo-ries, I vividly and thankfully recall your own long and close friendship with him, marked as it was, by a very special ap-proachability, a warm intimacy and a welcome regard. He spoke always of the inspiration and the knowledge with which his meetings with you, each time that he visited his birthplace in Ireland, were enriched. He felt for you the affec-tion and admiring respect of a privileged disciple.[41]

Mrs Herzog asked de Valera to contribute a chapter to a book which was being published in honour of her late husband.[42] De Valera, because of his position as President, reluctantly felt obliged to refuse the invitation.

To those who knew de Valera well, the gesture by the Irish

Jewish community had a deep personal impact. De Valera, for many years after the civil war a pariah in Irish society, had forged a deep friendship with leading members of the Jewish community during the War of Independence and afterwards. Those Irish Jews of an earlier generation, who knew the Fianna Fáil leader during the inter-war years, remembered with gratitude his support during the time of the Blueshirts and the period of fascist and nazi triumph in Europe. But for all his closeness to the Jewish community, de Valera's visit to the German minister following the death of Hitler in May 1945 was, and will, never be forgotten.

Cearbhall Ó Dálaigh and the Jewish community
The Jewish community also had cause to feel very grateful to another Irish person who had once been Attorney General in the postwar Fianna Fáil government. Born and reared in Bray, Cearbhall Ó Dálaigh – Irish scholar, journalist, Attorney General, Chief Justice and later a member of the EEC Court of Justice – was known to be a lifelong friend of the Jewish community in Dublin. When asked by Gabriel Fallon in a letter on 20 February 1967 to become the first patron of the newly founded Ireland-Israel Friendship League, he wrote: 'Yes, it will be an honour to lend a hand. Yes.'[43] In 1971, he was invited to contribute the foreword to Louis Hyman's *The Jews of Ireland – From Earliest Times to the Year 1910*. He did so with great diffidence:

> Have you not, at some time or other, when sitting in a theatre, eagerly awaiting the beginning of the play, felt a sense of annoyance as an uncostumed non-actor has stepped brashly through the curtains and begun to chatter about something or other? The writer of a foreward is just such an uncostumed non-actor, and is, equally, a source of annoyance. … It is a privilege to be permitted to share a little, however unworthily, in the permanence which, I don't doubt, Louis Hyman's book will achieve.[44]

Ó Dálaigh became President of Ireland in 1974 and was to hold that position for two years. On the day of his inauguration at Dublin Castle on 19 December 1974, he made time to attend divine service in the Adelaide Road Synagogue, Dublin, to mark the occasion. He was conducted to a seat of honour by District Justice Herman Good, by Hubert Wine and by Maurice Abrahamson of the Jewish Representative Council. The Chief Rabbi, Isaac Cohen, said in his address that the new President was no stranger to the Jewish community:

> Since his early youth he shared with many of our co-religionists the joys and the adventures, the anxieties and the hopes that have been experienced in our own Jewish life. His passionate love of learning, his breadth of humanity and his admiration of the achievements and hopes of the State of Israel have fashioned unbreakable ties of affection, esteem and honour in the hearts of the Jewish citizens of this great country.[45]

The remarks of Chief Rabbi Cohen merely reflected the fact that the new President had many personal friends in the Irish Jewish community. He was to remain a good friend of that community throughout his short presidency. Resigning on 22 October 1976 following an incident in which the then Minister for Defence spoke intemperately about the incumbent, he retired to Sneem, County Kerry. He died suddenly at home as a result of a heart attack on 21 March 1978. The Jewish community was represented at his funeral in Sneem by the Chief Rabbi Dr Isaac Cohen. The latter angered some members of the Jewish community because he stood outside St Michael's Church, not being permitted to enter a building where there was a dead body.[46]

Anti-Semitism and rebuilding the Jewish Community
in the 1960s and 1970s

Throughout the history of the Irish state a succession of talented chief rabbis had sought to provide unified leadership for the community:

Isaac Herzog 1918-1937
Immanuel Jakobovits 1949-1959
Isaac Cohen 1959-1979

David Rosen 1979-1984
Simon Harris 1993-1994
Gavin Broder 1996 –

Rabbi Cohen, who has been mentioned above, succeeded Jakobovits and spent over twenty years in Ireland – longer than Herzog. But the 1960s and 1970s were years of numerical decline for the community which did not see an end to anti-semitism in Ireland. An opinion poll published in 1977 concluded:

In summary, therefore, the evidence presented in this section has established the existence of a moderate degree of anti-semitic prejudice in Dublin. The pattern of this prejudice is along classical lines, i.e. the negative monetary and religious myths are still believed by a significant percentage of Dublin adults.[47]

The table of findings is worth reproducing in full

ANTI-SEMITIC SCALE BY TOTAL SAMPLE[48]

Introduction: 'Well, now, could we go on to talk about other religions. With regard to the Jews would you agree or disagree?'

Statement	Agree	Don't Know	Dis-agree	P-Score*	No.
1. That it would be good for the country to have many Jews in positions of responsibility in business	45.6	12.5	**41.9**	94.3	2,291
2. That Jews are a bad influence on Christian culture and civilization	**11.2**	5.6	83.2	28.0	2,290
3. That Jews have moral standards when dealing with each other, but with Christians they are ruthless and unscrupulous	**22.2**	10.8	67.1	55.1	2,288
4. That it is wrong for Jews and Christians to intermarry	**27.7**	6.1	66.2	61.6	2,290

Statement	Agree	Don't Know	Dis- agree	P-Score*	No.
5. That golf clubs or similar organisa- tions are justified in denying member- ship to a person because he or she is a Jew	**5.2**	2.0	92.8	12.5	2,290
6. That Jews as a people are to blame for the crucifixion of Christ	**15.8**	8.5	75.7	40.0	2,283
7. That Jews do not take a proper interest in community problems and government	**29.3**	15.9	54.8	74.5	2,278
8. That Jewish power and control in money matters is far out of proportion to the number of Jews	**57.3**	17.6	25.1	132.2	2,289
9. That Jews are behind the money lending rackets in Dublin	**49.2**	22.8	28.0	121.3	2,291
10. That we should encourage Irish Jews just as much as any- body else to take up positions of importance in Irish society	84.6	4.1	**11.3**	26.7	2,290
Scale P-Score				64.6	

*P-Score = 100 (M-1)
Note: Negative scores are in bold

The most negative responses were to items which had com- mercial or financial implications (See Nos. 1, 8 and 9). That was very much in line with the negative stereotypes of Jews. Some 60% surveyed agreed that Jews were over-represented in the control of money matters. Only 25% disagreed with that view.

The survey concludes:

> Therefore, it seems reasonable to conclude that this except-
> ionally high percentage of agreement with an unsubstantiated
> allegation against the Jews, may be attributed to anti-Semitic
> prejudice and the acceptance by the vast majority of respon-
> dents of the common stereotypical view of the Jews as the
> controllers of money matters today.[49]

That is borne out by the answer to question nine which saw
49.2 pc of the sample agree with the view that the Jews were behind the money lending rackets in Dublin. (Only 28% disagreed.)

The author of the survey felt that particular attention had
also to be paid to the answer to question six: 'The Jews as a people are to blame for the crucifixion of Christ.' That 'belief' ling-
ered among one-sixth of the sample and was denied by only
three quarters of those polled. It is concluded:

> For a minority, therefore, to be convicted of deicide, or the
> 'killing of Christ', is most serious in a society like Ireland. The
> evidence concerning the ascription of blame to the Jews as a
> people for the crucifixion of Christ merits serious attention.[50]

No question was asked directly on the Holocaust in this survey. But overall, its findings revealed a level of anti-Semitism
which might not have been so readily acknowledged in Irish
society. The 1977 survey was conducted eight years after 2,221
Catholic bishops had promulgated in 1965 the document *Nostra
Aetate* ('In Our Time') which was the Council's *Declaration on the
Relationship of the Church to Non-Christian Religions*.[51] *Nostra
Aetate* repudiated and deplored 'all hatreds, persecutions and
displays of anti-semitism directed against Jews at any time and
from any source'. Pope John XXIII had acted earlier to remove
some of the more blatant forms of the 'teaching of contempt'
against Jews and Judaism which had found their way into the
Roman rite. He had removed the phrase 'perfidious Jews' from
the Good Friday prayers. Paul VI revised the prayer, which became one 'For the Jews' rather than 'For the conversion of the
Jews'.[52] *Nostra Aetate* was implemented in Ireland in accordance
with the 1974 Vatican guidelines for Catholic-Jewish Relations.

Dialogue between Christians and Jews in the country continues to be conducted by a group of highly dedicated religious and lay people.

Dr Micheál MacGréil published an undated study on prejudice in Irish society in 1996. The survey registered a relatively high level of prejudice towards Jews in the more rural areas of Ireland. A significant minority, 20%, still regarded Jews as being responsible for the crucifixion of Christ. The 'money-matters' stereotype had declined since 1972/3. He concluded cautiously that 'on balance, the situation is moderately positive with room for improvement' on the question of anti-Semitism.[53]

Ultra right wing groups
Nevertheless, anti-Semitism, which had never been a central driving force in Irish politics and society, continued to manifest itself in the latter part of the century in the ranks of rightist Catholic groups and diminutive branches of British neo-fascist organisations.

A small number of ultra right wing groups have, from time to time, established themselves in Ireland. But they have been as unrepresentative as their actions have been inconsequential. The proximity of England meant that Dublin was sometimes seen as a convenient outpost in which to locate anti-Semitic printing operations. This was so in the 1970s in the case of the National Socialist Irish Workers' Party. Working out of a house in a poor area of Dublin, the NSIWP sought the 'repatriation' of Jews, Asians and Blacks, stating that if that was not done the Irish would lose their distinctive culture.[54] An off-shoot of a British neo-fascist organisation, its activities were closely observed by the gardaí. It attracted no more than a handful of followers in the capital.

In the 1980s, Cork also had a short-lived neo-nazi organisation, again working out of a house in one of the poorer parts of the city. But Ireland has not proved a very fertile recruiting ground for international neo-nazi organisations. Neo-fascist groups operating in Ireland have recycled the literature containing the stereotypical belief systems of the far right.

Throughout the post-war period in Ireland, therefore, there was a need to address certain deficits in the civic culture concerning attitudes to minorities. Where sensitivity developed in this area, it was substantially in reference to the crisis in Northern Ireland. From the 1960s onwards, Dr Garret FitzGerald and other leading politicians sought to emphasise the diversity of the Irish historical tradition and the growing pluralism of that society. The question of anti-Semitism is a matter which ought to receive greater reflection and action in the years to come.

Irish Jews and the wider community
Jakobovits had referred in the 1950s to the diffidence of Irish Jews about becoming involved in Irish politics. That was no longer the case by the 1970s. For example, Gerald Goldberg was a distinguished member of the minuscule Jewish community in Cork and an independent member of the corporation for eight years. He joined Fianna Fáil and in 1977 he became the first Jewish Lord Mayor of Cork. Later, he commented sadly but accurately that he was the first but also 'very likely its last'.[55]

There were three Jewish members in the 29th Dáil Éireann between 1992 and 1997. Ben Briscoe was a member of Fianna Fáil. Mervyn Taylor, a lawyer and member of the Labour Party, was Minister for Equality and Law Reform. Alan Shatter, who is a lawyer by profession, was a Fine Gael TD – the first in the history of the party. The Blueshirts of the 1930s cast a long shadow in the Irish Jewish community.[56] Attracted by the ideas of the liberal wing of the party in the 1970s, he broke with tradition.

A brief social audit of the contribution of Jews to Irish life reveals that the community has contributed disproportionately to its numbers. In the world of learning the contributions of Dr Jacob Weingreen, Professor of Hebrew in TCD, are notable, as is the literary criticism of A. J. (Con) Leventhal from the same university. The names of Solomons and Abrahamson have been very prominent in the medical profession. Other Jewish families associated with medicine were Eppel and Freedman.

Michael Noyk and Bernard Shillman were distinguished

members of the Irish legal profession while Herman Good, Hubert Wine and Henry Baron served in the judiciary. Herman Good's legal practice had a large concentration of clients from very poor areas in the city.

The Minister for Equality and Law Reform, Mervyn Taylor, was very much in the legal reform tradition of both Wine and Good. Taylor's involvement in the Labour Party was largely instrumental in bringing him into active politics. Before retiring in 1997, he was responsible during his time as a minister in the 'Rainbow coalition' government for completing in November 1996 the report of the Commission on the Status of People with Disabilities. Taylor's department was also responsible for the passage of the Civil Legal Aid Act, the Powers of Attorney Act, the Employment Equality Act and the Equal Status Act. He was also involved in introducing measures to reduce the waiting time in law centres, the opening of a family mediation centre in Limerick, the support of marriage counselling services and a pilot childcare initiative.[57]

The list of prominent members of the Jewish community in the areas of learning, medicine and the law is indicative rather than exhaustive. The late Victor Waddington was a gallery owner and promoter of the arts in Ireland. He was responsible for discovering and promoting Irish artists like Colin Middleton and George Campbell. The painter Gerald Davis also runs a gallery in Dublin. Harry Kernoff, Estella F. Solomons and Stella Steyn were Jewish painters of distinction. The German graphic designer and calligrapher, Elizabeth Friedlander, who spent most of her life working in England, retired to Kinsale and died in the home of her close friends, Sheila and Gerald Goldberg.[58] Dr Jack Eppel was a pioneer of Irish cinema. The civil servant Larry Elyan, who later went to Israel, was also a creative and innovative force in Irish theatre as is Carolyn Swift, a founder of the Pike Theatre in the 1950s.[59]

Hannah Berman was among the first novelists to emerge from the Jewish community in Dublin after the turn of the century. A few generations later, David Marcus, a former literary editor of the *Irish Press*, played an important role in the 1950s fostering young writers and poets. He continued that work as literary editor of the *Irish Press* in the 'New Irish Writing' page – the literary section of the *Irish Press*. Marcus is also the author of a collection of short stories entitled *Who ever heard of an Irish Jew and other short stories*[60] and the novel, *A Land not Theirs*.[61] His brother Louis Marcus is a distinguished film maker as is another member of the Jewish community, Louis Lentin.

In the world of music, Dina Copeman and the concert pianist Estelle Wine, sister of Judge Hubert Wine, must be mentioned, as might many others who have contributed to the intellectual, cultural and professional life of the state. Fr Michael O'Carroll, a Holy Ghost priest who has made a distinguished contribution to Jewish-Christian dialogue from the 1940s, states that the Jewish community had made a contribution to the life of the nation 'out of all proportion to its numbers'.[62]

Irish Government reaction to the Holocaust
President Ó Dálaigh's excellent relationship with the Jewish community was sustained by all other Irish presidents, Douglas Hyde, Seán T. O'Kelly, Éamon de Valera, Erskine Childers and Dr Patrick Hillery. Mrs Mary Robinson, elected President of Ireland in 1990, has done much to demonstrate in a practical way her deep awareness of the suffering of Jews in the twentieth century. In the year of the sixtieth anniversary of the liberation of the death camps, she visited Auschwitz-Birkenau and laid a wreath at the Death Wall. Before leaving the camp, she wrote in the visitors' book:

> On my own behalf and of the people Ireland I have come to pay deep respect, to honour the victims, and to remember the terrible deeds in this place. We must always remember the inhumanity of man to men, to women and to children. Only if we remember will we remain eternally vigilant. Sadly, that vigilance is needed in our world today.[63]

Asked by a Polish journalist at Birkenau whether the concentrations camps should not be preserved but destroyed completely, she responded:

I do not share that view. I believe that it is very important
that not only the place would remain, but that it would remain as authentically as it remains at the moment. I know
that it is difficult, and I know that for some families in particular it must be almost too painful to come. We must come
here. We must take on board what happened here. We must
do it because it must not be allowed to recur. And yet, we
know in our hearts that the ingredients of racism, of anti-
Semitism, of ethnic hatred are there, and none of us can be
complacent or feel that we don't need places like this. Yet we
do. It is most important that you keep and you value as I do
the opportunity – that is, to see at first hand the capacity for
inhumanity that is with us – so that it may bring out the capacity for compassion, for tolerance, for reaching out to each
other and for being open to each other.[64]

She also said:

I know that this is a very special place for all Jewish communities, and I thought of our own Jewish community in
Ireland, our small but beloved Jewish community. Some of
them have lost relatives, close family, here.[65]

President Robinson rightly said that it was important not just
to remember, but to feel chastened: 'this is not something that
we can say comfortably, it is of the past, it is over.' She went on:

Unfortunately, there can always be a resurgence of racism, of
anti-Semitism, of ethnic violence. We see it in Europe, sadly.
We see it elsewhere in the world. I am glad to come here as
the first President of Ireland to visit Poland. It was important
for me that I came here.[66]

Senior Irish politicians shared President Robinson's anxiety
not to allow 1995 to pass without showing Irish solidarity with
the victims of the Holocaust. The Taoiseach, Mr John Bruton,
took steps to mark officially the liberation of Bergen-Belsen.[67]
Despite initial confusion caused by the choice of Saturday 15
April 1995 – the Jewish Sabbath and the first day of Passover –
the date of the ceremony was rearranged.[68]

The Fine Gael TD, Alan Shatter, reviewed at that time the

Irish government's wartime policy towards refugees and commented:

> There has never been a state ceremony in Ireland to commemorate the 6 million Jews who were murdered in the Holocaust. There has never been any official expression of regret from any Irish government at the state's refusal to admit into Ireland the many Jews fleeing from Nazi terror.[69]

A joint commemoration of the liberation of Bergen-Belsen by the Jewish Community and the Ireland-Israel Friendship League was announced for 26 April. Mr Bruton was invited to attend the ceremony and to give an address. Included in the attendance were Holocaust survivors resident in Ireland, as well as the children and grandchildren of survivors. The congregation of 400 was drawn from all the churches, business and labour associations, and other civic groups.[70] In his speech, Mr Bruton said: 'We in Ireland have not been immune from the bigotry and the indifference which manifested themselves in Europe this century.' He acknowledged that official Irish archives had revealed that Ireland's doors 'were not freely open to those families and individuals fleeing from persecution and death.' He said that some people

> did find refuge and comfort in Ireland, but their numbers were not very great. We must acknowledge the consequences of this indifference. As a society we have become more willing to accept our responsibility to respond to events beyond our shores.[71]

He continued:

> Tonight, on behalf of the Irish government and people I honour the memory of those millions of European Jews who died in the Holocaust.[72]

The Taoiseach stated that fifty years after the liberation of the death camps 'the recognition of the colossal evil enacted in these places is branded deep in the moral conscience of modern man'. He pointed out that the Holocaust was 'first and foremost a crime against the Jewish people; more fundamentally it was a crime against all humanity. Its memory must always be kept alive. I would again quote Primo Levi when he said, "It happened, therefore it can happen again." Too much in today's world tells us that we have yet to grasp the full significance of this fact.'[73]

Those sentiments, held strongly by all political parties in the country, have influenced two relevant pieces of legislation – the Prohibition of Incitement to Hatred Act (1989) and a Refugee Act in 1997.

In the latter part of the 1990s, the refugee problem in Ireland has intensified in a manner reminiscent of the 1930s. The Irish Refugee Council record that the numbers seeking asylum in Ireland increased by 278% between 1995 and 1996. There were 1,179 asylum seekers in 1996. The number was 39 in 1992.[74] That new situation will – in a Europe where racism is on the increase – continue to test the tolerance of Irish society.

In twentieth-century Ireland, the Jewish community – north and south of the border – have played an important role in all aspects of Irish life. They will not be present in such great numbers in the Ireland of the early twenty-first century. But the Judeo-dimension of Irish identity will survive as long as the words of that most famous fictional Jewish Irishman, Leopold Bloom:

> 'Force, hatred, history, all that. That's not life for men and women, insult and hatred.'[75]

Notes:
1. Mark Lieberman, 'The Jews of Northern Ireland: Living in Peace in a Troubled Land', *Jewish Monthly,* March 1989, p 19.
2. See Table.
3. *Census of Population of Northern Ireland, 1991.* Figures kindly supplied by Dr Caroline Windrum, Institute of Irish Studies, Queen's University, Belfast.
4. Andy Pollak, 'Dublin's Jewish Community is here for the long haul despite its decline,' in *The Irish Times,* 7 March 1995.
5. Stanley Waterman, 'On the South Side of the Liffey', *The Jewish Quarterly,* Spring, 1987, p 28.

6. J. J. Sexton and R. O'Leary, 'Factors affecting Population Decline in Minority Religious Communities in the Republic of Ireland', *Building Trust in Ireland – Studies Commissioned by the Forum for Peace and Reconciliation* (The Blackstaff Press, Belfast, 1995), pp 307-309.

7. ibid., pp 307-309.

8. Stanley Waterman, 'On the South Side of the Liffey', *The Jewish Quarterly*, Spring, 1987, p 30.

9. Immanuel Jakobovits, *Journal of a Rabbi* (W.H. Allen, London, 1967), pp 57-60.

10. ibid., p 54.

11. The areas of exception were Zionist organisation and youth work; ibid., p 55.

12. Information based on interviews conducted on my behalf in 1996/7, Dr Caroline Windrum, Institute of Irish Studies, Queen's University, Belfast.

13. Information supplied to me by Dr Caroline Windrum, Institute of Irish Studies, Queen's University, Belfast.

14. Stanley Waterman, 'Changing Residential Patterns of the Dublin Jewish Community', *Irish Geography*, Vol. 14, 1981, pp 43-44.

15. ibid., p 44.

16. Immanuel Jakobovits, op. cit., pp 57-60.

17. Asher Benson, 'Jewish Genealogy in Ireland', *Aspects of Irish Genealogy – Proceedings of the 1st Irish Genealogical Congress*, p 21. Four out of every five Jewish children of school-age, of whom there were about 500 in the 1950s, received regular Jewish instruction, according to Jakobovits. There was a strong attendance at Zion schools. There were fifteen Jewish youth organisations in Dublin during that decade. Members of the Jewish community going on to third level education usually attended Trinity College.

18 Asher Benson, op. cit., p 21.

19. The Dublin Maccabi which opened its own sports grounds on 25 May 1952. Immanuel Jakobovits, op. cit., pp 57-60.

20. Immanuel Jakobovits, op. cit., pp 64.

21. He also stated that the Elliman family had recently secured a controlling interest in the Royal, Metropole, Gaiety, and Savoy theatres in Dublin as well as having theatrical interests in Cork and Limerick. Vinton Chapin to State Department, 17 May 1949, G 84, State Department, Ireland (security segregated records), National Archives, Washington D.C.

22. Dermot Keogh, 'The Role of the Catholic Church in the Republic of Ireland 1922-1995', in *Building Trust in Ireland – Studies Commissioned by the Forum for Peace and Reconciliation* (The Blackstaff Press, Belfast, 1996), p 137.

23. Andree Sheehy Skeffington, *Skeff – A Life of Owen Sheehy Skeffington 1909-1970* (Lilliput Press, Dublin, 1991), pp 141-162.

24. See Department of Justice, S13/50/1, National Archives, Dublin.

25. ibid.

26. ibid.

27. ibid.

28. See Dermot Keogh, 'The Role of the Catholic Church in the Republic of Ireland 1922-1995', in *Building Trust in Ireland*, op. cit., pp 134-142.

29. The Fethard-on-Sea case in the 1950s, involving the children of a mixed marriage in County Wexford, provided negative headlines for a short time in 1957. See Dermot Keogh, 'The Role of the Catholic Church in the Republic of Ireland 1922-1995', in *Building Trust in Ireland*, op. cit., pp 142-149.

30. Immanuel Jakobovits, op. cit., p 270.

31. ibid.

32. His son, Ben, succeeded him in the Dáil in 1965. The latter also became Lord Mayor of Dublin on 5 July 1988. See Ted Nealon, *Nealon's Guide to the 27th Dáil and Seanad – Election 1992* (Gill and Macmillan, Dublin, 1993).

33. 'Eamon de Valera and Israel', file 844, Éamon de Valera papers, Franciscan Archives, Killiney, Co Dublin.

34. *Lusk Leader,* 15 May 1965. File 844, Éamon de Valera papers, Franciscan Archives, Killiney, Co Dublin.

35. *The Irish Press,* 17 August 1966.

36. Eshkol to Abrahamson, 18 August 1966, Éamon de Valera papers, files 844, Franciscan archives, Killiney, Co Dublin.

37. Eshkol to Abrahamson, 18 August 1966, Éamon de Valera papers, files 844, Franciscan archives, Killiney, Co Dublin.

38. Herzog to Abrahamson, 18 August 1966, Éamon de Valera papers, files 844, Franciscan archives, Killiney, Co Dublin.

39. Max Nurock speech, 18 August 1966, file 844, Éamon de Valera papers, Franciscan archives, Killiney, Co.Dublin.

40. *The Jewish Chronicle,* 14 September 1966; cutting in file 844, Éamon de Valera papers, Franciscan Archives, Killiney, Co Dublin.

41. File 844, Éamon de Valera papers, Franciscan Archives, Killiney, Co Dublin.

42. Obituary, *The London Times,* 13 March 1972.

43. See correspondence in Cearbhall Ó Dálaigh file, Box 25, Irish Jewish Museum archives, Dublin.

44. Cearbhall Ó Dálaigh, 'Foreword', in Louis Hyman, *The Jews of Ireland – From Earliest Times to the Year 1910* (Irish University Press, Shannon, 1972), xv.

45. 'Jewish Community honours President', *The Irish Times,* 20 December 1974.

46. See photograph and caption, p 1, *The Irish Times,* 23 March 1978. The view was strongly expressed to me by a leading member of the Jewish community that he might have allowed the community to be represented by somebody else who would have joined the funeral service inside the church.

47. Micheál Mac Gréil, *Prejudice and Tolerance in Ireland* (Leinster Leader, Kildare, 1978), p 525 and p 333 for the table.

48. ibid., p 333.

49. ibid., p 333

50. ibid., pp 333-335.

51. Eugene J. Fisher, 'Nostra Aetate, for Our Times and for the Future', in Eugene J. Fisher *et al.* (eds.), *Twenty Years of Jewish-Catholic Relations* (Paulist Press, New York, 1986), p 1.

52. Eugene J. Fisher, 'The Roman Liturgy and Catholic-Jewish Relations since the Second Vatican Council', in Eugene J. Fisher *et al.* (eds.), *Twenty years of Jewish-Catholic Relations*, op. cit., pp 135-138.

53. Micheál MacGréil, *Prejudice in Ireland Revisited* (St Patrick's College, Maynooth, 1996), p 223.

54. 'Irish Nazis: Why Dublin is a Fascist Haven,' *In Dublin*, 24 July, No. 259, pp 24-27.

55. Gerald Y. Goldberg, 'The Freeman of Cork,' *The Cork Review* (special issue on Seán Ó Faoláin 1900-1991), 1991, pp 58-59.

56. Herman Good, later a distinguished member of the Irish judiciary, stood unsuccessfully for the Labour Party, in 1944. The Jewish community has produced a number of very fine athletes. For example, Bethel Solomons, later master of the Rotunda Hospital, was capped ten times for Ireland in rugby. Louis Bookman played soccer for Ireland four times between 1914 and 1922, and Judge Hubert Wine played table tennis for Ireland. Information taken from the Jewish Museum, Dublin.

57. See *Activities of Government Departments – Reports from Departmental Press Officers* (Government Information Service, Dublin, 1997), pp 62-64.

58. Joe Burns, 'Visually speaking', *The Cork Examiner*, 29 February 1988. Elizabeth Friedlander was also a skilled wood engraver. She designed book jackets for Penguin. See Sheila and Gerald Goldberg Friedlander collection, Boole Library, University College Cork.

59. See Gerald Davis, 'On being a Jew in Ireland', *Everyman*, No. 1, 1968, pp 109-110.

60. Published by Bantam, London, 1988.

61. Published by Corgi, London, 1986.

62. Interview with Fr Michael O'Carroll, Blackrock College, Dublin, July 1996.

63. *The Irish Times*, 24 June 1994.

64. ibid.

65. ibid.

66. President Robinson recalled that an Irish Government Minister, Mervyn Taylor had lost family members there.

67. His office felt it appropriate to choose the actual day of liberation, 15 April. On the personal initiative of the Taoiseach, invitations to a short ceremony at the War Memorial in Islandbridge, were sent out. This was to be followed by a reception in the Royal Hospital in Kilmainham. See Geraldine Kennedy, 'Ceremony Changed after Passover clash revealed – Belsen to be commemorated,' in *The Irish Times*, 8 April 1995.

68. The Taoiseach was very quick to change the date. His office said that he had consulted a 'senior member of the Jewish community' before doing so. That may have been his party colleague and Minister for Equality and Law Reform, Mr Mervyn Taylor, who is Jewish. Another Fine Gael member of the Dáil, Alan Shatter, who is also Jewish, said that he was disappointed that the Taoiseach did not contact him beforehand and that the embarrassment could have been avoided. See *The Irish Times*, 8 April 1995.

69. *The Irish Times*, 21 April 1995.

70. See *The Ireland-Israel Friendship League Newsletter*, Vol. 1, No. 2, September 1995.

71. ibid.

72. Bruton also said: 'I also recall the gypsies and homosexual community who were marked down for extermination and all those who were persecuted for resisting the Nazi tyranny ... I am also humble to be here when we have with us some of those who have borne witness personally to the horror and reality of the Holocaust.' See *The Ireland-Israel Friendship League Newsletter*, Vol. 1, No. 2, September 1995.

73. Text of John Bruton's speech, 26 April 1995, kindly supplied by the Government Information Services.

74. Martin Wall, '20 million pound cost to maintain refugees', *The Sunday Tribune*, 20 April 1997.

75. James Joyce, *Ulysses*, annotated students' edition, (Penguin, London, 1992), pp 432-433.

Sectarianism and the Churches:
The Legacy and the Challenge

Joseph Liechty

The Christian churches in Ireland enter a new millennium lumbered by the ball and chain called sectarianism. Forged initially in the Reformation-era struggle for religious and political supremacy, sectarianism has taken different forms over the centuries, overt and hidden, flagrant and polite, individual and corporate. While still capable of generating spectacular acts of hatred and violence, sectarianism in its day-to-day manifestations is perhaps most remarkable for being so widespread as to be invisible. Sectarianism silently persuades us by its perseverance and pervasive presence that its dragging effects are simply the way things are, must be, and always will be.

Although the 1990s have seen heartening signs that the churches are increasingly unwilling to carry this weight, the work of challenging sectarianism is in its early stages, still requiring rudimentary tools. One fundamental problem, for example, is that we have typically approached sectarianism from a stance of blaming others and absolving ourselves. Thus citizens of Britain and the Republic of Ireland see sectarianism as a Northern Ireland problem, conveniently ignoring the fact that the people of Northern Ireland are suffering under a legacy bequeathed to them by processes implicating the whole of these islands. Examples can be multiplied endlessly, because everyone always has someone else to blame. One set of tools required, therefore, is ways of thinking about responsibility for sectarianism that can engage 'us' as well as 'them'. The following reflection on sectarianism as a system is one attempt to address the problem.

Sectarianism as a system

Since January 1995, Cecilia Clegg and I have run the Moving Beyond Sectarianism project for the Irish School of Ecumenics. While an understanding of sectarianism as a system has been part of our work from the beginning, we have found it increasingly important to stress the systemic nature of sectarianism. We might pose the problem as follows: much thinking about sectarianism is faulty because we take a solely personal approach to a problem that is both personal and systemic. When thinking about sectarianism, we typically begin with personal attitudes and personal actions. Thus we absolve a person of responsibility, we think, when we say, 'She doesn't have a sectarian bone in her body.' In one sense, this concern with the personal is not only appropriate, we need more of it, not less. At the same time, however, a too exclusively personal approach fails to take seriously enough the systemic issues around sectarianism. To pose the problem another way: a sectarian system can be maintained by people who, individually, do not have a sectarian bone in their bodies. Some reflection on the nature and origin of the sectarian system will show how this paradox comes to pass.

Sectarianism is a system that works sometimes with sledge hammer directness and brutality, sometimes with great subtlety. We were struck by the juxtaposition of these modes in stories told in a Catholic group we worked with in the autumn of 1998. A priest told of his horror at standing across the street, powerless to intervene, while an IRA man pumped bullets into the head of an RUC man fallen at his feet. That is the sledge hammer. In the same session, a woman spoke of the effects of an annual Orange parade in the neighbourhood where she grew up. As she told the story, this was not a rowdy parade, and indeed nothing particularly dramatic ever happened. And yet that annual event, always accompanied by her family staying in their house and quietly hoping that nothing would happen, generated in her an unspoken but ever-present sense of intimidation and limitation that shaped her life: where she would go, obviously, and whom she would befriend, but more subtle and internal limitations as well – a reserve and caution that did not always show, but that always shaped those encounters she did have with Protestants. As she spoke, however, what seemed to distress her most was her sense, as a middle-aged mother of older children, that without ever intending or even realising it, she had somehow passed on the same limitations to her children. In one sense little or nothing happened, and yet the quietly destructive effects could shape a life and pass silently to a new generation. The system can be that subtle.

In its formative days, the 1500s and onwards, sectarianism knew little of subtlety. Sectarianism requires division, in particular antagonised division, so in the beginning sectarianism worked with bold strokes: big hate, big violence, gross injustice. In the beginning, then, sectarianism generated and fed on events like the Elizabethan Wars in Ireland, plantation, the 1641 Rising, Cromwell, the Williamite Wars, penal laws, and so on. And since this is not just any antagonised division, it is sectarianism, it requires a religious contribution.

It requires an English Protestant officer reflecting on a sixteenth-century military campaign in Ulster in these terms: 'how godly a dede it is to overthrowe so wicked a race [as the Irish] the world may judge: for my part I thinke there canot be a greater sacryfice to God.'

It requires that Catholic resistance to such logic should be framed in religious terms, so that when in 1579 James Fitzmaurice Fitzgerald returned to Ireland from four years on the continent to mount a campaign against the English crown, he should declare that the 'only object' of his campaign was to 'secure the administration of Christ's Sacraments to a Catholic people in a Catholic rite', and his landing party should be led by two Franciscans bearing a banner blessed by the Pope, then by a bishop in full regalia, then by seven hundred soldiers paid for by the Pope. Fitzmaurice himself bore a letter from the Pope urging Irish Catholics to rise against the heretics and promising all who did 'the same plenary indulgence and remission of sins that those receive who fight against the Turks and for the recovery of the Holy Land.' These were the terms of holy war.

It requires that in the 1641 Rising, the Old English and the Irish parties, who could not unite under any other banner, should join together as the Confederate Catholics of Ireland, and that their leader, Owen Roe O'Neill, should return to Ireland with another letter from another Pope, this one praising O'Neill's 'excelling fervour, that is, your constancy against the heretics' and offering a blessing to all 'who would help the cause of the Catholics'.

It requires in return that Cromwell should publicly defend his radical violence as godly vengeance.

It requires that the Catholic, Presbyterian, and Anglican churches in the seventeenth century should each regard themselves as the one true church, that each should align itself with a political cause, and that each should, under the shared conviction that error has no rights, seek victory and dominance over the other parties.

Neither can such matters be dismissed as distant history. These sixteenth- and seventeenth-century dynamics have been reflected in this century, even if in milder form.

Sectarianism requires, therefore, that Pádraig Pearse's revolutionary thought should involve a heretical union of Christianity and nationalism.

It requires that Protestant resistance to home rule, sealed in the 1912 Solemn League and Covenant, should involve the church-blessed threat of violent resistance.

It requires that the two new states created by the partition of Ireland should function to a large extent as a Protestant state and a Catholic state.

It requires Cardinal MacRory announcing in the 1930s that the Protestant traditions really are not Christian churches at all.

It requires discrimination against Catholics in Northern Ireland, with Protestants turning a blind eye or supporting it.

It requires Pope Pius XII rejecting religious liberty and re-affirming that error has no rights in the 1950s, so that until the Second Vatican Council opts for religious liberty in the 1960s, Protestant fears that 'home rule is Rome rule' have a rational basis in official Catholic doctrine.

While no match for its Reformation-era predecessors, this kind of sectarianism is still relatively direct and simple.

Sectarianism still nurtures injustice and violence, which remain its most potent fuels. The shock waves sent out by violence have a particular power to deepen and strengthen the sectarian divide. But the sectarian system, now long established, no longer requires large amounts of such comparatively exotic fuels to maintain itself. Just an occasional act of violence will do, because the sectarian system disposes us to judge others by the worst actions of the worst elements of 'their' community. Nor do motivations for the violence matter much. When accused of sectarianism, gross or subtle, most people turn first to their intentions and motivations to absolve themselves, but the victims or potential victims are not listening, and for good reason. Under threat, all we are interested in knowing is where the threat comes from. And this is a rational response to a real threat – we do not avoid some areas or situations at some times out of a paranoid fear that everyone is out to get us, but out of a reasonable fear that someone might be. This is no more than prudence, the self-preservation instinct at work.

And yet sectarianism has become a system so efficient that it can take our sane and rational responses to a situation which it has generated and use them to further deepen sectarianism. For an example, we need look no further than one of the principal structural responses to the violence of the last thirty years, the increasing movement from mixed residential situations to living exclusively among our own. No one could in any way be faulted for doing so, and yet the corporate effect of these individually sensible and blameless movements is to reinforce sectarianism still further. This is only to look at the most obvious responses to sectarianism, of course. Others may have stopped short of physically withdrawing from mixed situations, whether residential, vocational, or social, while withdrawing in spirit. Our trust has been violated, so we redraw the boundaries and hold ourselves back from unseen but effective limits. This too is an entirely understandable response to sectarianism. And here we might pause to marvel – for a system that can maintain itself by feeding on logical responses to situations it has itself created is a wonder of adaptation.

When good people do not act

In fact, the efficiency of the sectarian system goes at least two steps further. First, sectarianism does not really require any direct, active response at all from most of us; it simply requires that we do nothing about it. 'Comparative sectarianism' is the simple and efficient mechanism the sectarian system has established for keeping us passive or at least keeping our protests ineffectual. We are inclined to approach sectarianism by drawing lines between them and us, and since we can always find a 'them' out there whose actions can be plausibly construed as worse than ours, we can justify ourselves in identifying 'them' as the real sectarian problem. While distinctions between levels and grades of sectarianism are important, the problem is that everyone can find someone worse than themselves, so no one is ever responsible. This buck never stops passing. We may even rail against sectarian abuses and therefore regard ourselves as anti-sectarian, but because they are always someone else's abuses we are attacking, the sectarian system can readily absorb our criticisms and carry on undisturbed. In the meantime, the comparative sectarianism approach means that the systemic features of sectarianism are rarely even addressed.

Second, the sectarian system can sometimes use even our best efforts to build itself up. Given the church-related concentration of our work in the Moving Beyond Sectarianism project, we see this most crucially in the way that sectarianism feeds on Christians' religiously motivated boundary maintenance. We choose to worship, educate, and marry almost exclusively among our own. Our motivation is not to be sectarian, it is to build strong communities, but because our efforts fall within the boundaries set by sectarianism, our best pastoral efforts can end up strengthening the sectarian divide. Ironically, strong communities are and will be crucial to challenging sectarianism. And yet so long as the churches see challenging the sectarian divide as a marginal responsibility, or no responsibility at all, or a responsibility we will address when everything else has been settled, the sectarian system will go on employing well-intentioned, positive, community-building activities as sustenance for itself.

So it is that the sectarian system, born from gross violence and what most people would now see as unapologetic injustice, can now maintain itself on a diet consisting largely of our rational responses, understandable comparisons, good intentions, and positive actions. A system so impressively efficient is not going to disappear simply because we are now enjoying paramilitary ceasefires, more or less, and a measure of political progress, however fragile. It will need to be challenged, by Christians, their churches, and others, in a range of creative ways and for a long time to come.

Reflections

This meditation on sectarianism as a system has become a standard feature in virtually every presentation we give, or group work session we lead, whether for a local cross-community group or a national gathering of church leaders. For a variety of reasons, it is proving to be a useful tool.

Readers will have noticed that we consistently and strongly reify sectarianism as a living and even wilful entity. We may initially have done this occasionally and casually, but for several reasons it has long since become a deliberate approach.

First, a reified presentation of sectarianism reflects people's experience. Take, for example, the setting from which this reflection on sectarianism as a system first emerged. We were working for two weekends with a Catholic religious order and some of their key lay collaborators in a review of their ministry, thinking particularly about how they could address issues of sectarianism. An early session involved the group of fifteen to twenty people relating their personal experiences of sectarianism. As story after story revealed the contours, complexity, and sinister power of sectarianism, a numinous atmosphere settled over the group. Regrettably, however, the divinity evoked was a dark one, and the awe it inspired was enervating. Near the end of the session I made some fumbling, reifying remarks about the nature of the beast we were confronting. It sparked some recognition and interest, and after the session, some people asked me if I would elaborate. That night I wrote out a cruder version of the reflection on sectarianism as a system offered in this chapter, and the next morning I shared it with the group. What I said met with quiet but firm assent, and the mood changed. Having evoked, recognised, and named sectarianism, we could now get on, it seemed, with the business of challenging it. Since that weekend, this reflection on sectarianism as a system has to some extent played a similar role – a mix of focusing, bonding, and energising in virtually every group we have talked to or worked with. To date, this reflection has never been rejected. In fact it has never been challenged, even in part.

Second, by reifying sectarianism we mean to connect it to the biblical concept of principalities and powers, especially as mediated to us by Walter Wink's work on the powers (*Engaging the Powers: Discernment and Resistance in a World of Domination,* Minneapolis: Fortress Press, 1992). While we only make explicit use of this language in a few places in our written work, it consistently undergirds our thinking about sectarianism, as it does in this sectarianism-as-a-system passage. While sectarianism generates both concrete institutions and a correlating malign spirituality, the spiritual aspect is probably less apparent to modern sensibilities. It is most useful, therefore, to embrace a perspective that allows us to see that the struggle against sectarianism is 'against the rulers, against the authorities, against the cosmic powers of this present darkness, against the spiritual forces of evil in the heavenly place'. (Eph 6:12, NRSV) For many, Wink's treatment will help to bridge the gap between biblical and modern worldviews.

Third, reifying sectarianism provides us with what is so very difficult to come by in Northern Ireland: an agreed and shared enemy that we can struggle against together. People returning to Northern Ireland after long experience of the struggle against apartheid in South Africa bemoan the absence in Northern

Ireland of a broad and identifiable movement one can join to op-
pose a broad and identifiable evil. Reflecting on her observations
of sectarianism and inter-church relations in Northern Ireland, a
Reformed pastor from Romania recently commented that what
the North requires is a Communist dictatorship. Then we would
have a shared oppressor, and our clergy and others could get to
know, respect, like, and collaborate with each other in prison,
and even take those lessons back into day-to-day life, as happened in Romania. In the absence of such an unlikely blessing, a
reified sectarianism goes some way toward meeting the need.

Fourth, a reified sectarianism helps us in the delicate task of
assigning responsibility for sectarianism without, as our colleague Fran Porter put it, 'apportioning paralysing chunks of
blame'. The response we hope to evoke in those we work with
might be put like this: we face a problem of awesome power and
subtlety; there is no hiding from it and little innocence in the face
of it; it implicates us collectively and individually; let us join together to face it. Sometimes this happens, and sometimes this
sectarianism-as-a-system reflection seems to help it happen.

In addition to the reification of sectarianism, readers may
also have noticed a slippery use of 'we'. Sometimes 'we' refers to
Cecilia and me. Sometimes 'we' refers to something larger and
more vague, perhaps the people of Northern Ireland, perhaps
those who wish to challenge sectarianism. Sometimes it is un-
clear which use of 'we', the narrow or the broad, we intend.
Again, what may once have been an unconscious ambiguity has
become deliberate. We are both outsiders, Cecilia as a Scot with
an English accent and I many times over, as an American, a
Mennonite, and a Dubliner. Outsider status is in some ways crucial to our work, and if we did not have it, we might be tempted
to cultivate it. Being outsiders is not an unmixed blessing, however, so we also need to find ways to temper it. We have been
continually alert to what we call 'the shock of recognition' –
those occasions when the experience of Northern Ireland is not
only what we observe but also a mirror in which we see ourselves and our communities, perhaps in unexpected ways. As
'the shock of recognition' has become more 'the expectation of

recognition', a many-layered and ambiguous use of 'we' has come to seem an honest indication of the ways we are both outsiders and insiders. It is also one more way of cultivating that crucial sense of standing together, all of us implicated and yet determined to challenge a formidable opponent.

One of the things that makes this an exciting time to undertake this challenge is signs of an unprecedented, if still occasional and tentative, engagement of issues around sectarianism by the churches. Best of all, such activity is coming from diverse sectors of Christianity. Significant numbers of lay Christians of many denominations are finding ways to address sectarianism. The ecumenical movement has made an important contribution, including the ground-breaking inter-church Working Party on Sectarianism established by the Irish Inter-Church Meeting and the Irish School of Ecumenics' Moving Beyond Sectarianism project. No organisation is working more vitally and creatively, or with more people, on issues related to sectarianism than Evangelical Contribution on Northern Ireland (ECONI). Some Catholic religious orders are starting to address issues of sectarianism when reviewing their ministries. The Church of Ireland established a committee to conduct an audit of sectarianism within its own ranks. Their report, presented to the General Synod in May 1999, was widely criticised, mostly for not being decisive enough or wide-ranging enough. Perhaps many of us, operating from positions of relative comfort and safety and without responsibility for the consequences of what we propose, might have written a tougher, more coherent report. But any such criticisms do nothing to diminish the significance of what the Church of Ireland has done. No denomination has ever addressed sectarianism as an internal problem so directly and publicly, consequently helping to take discussion of sectarianism out of the realm of angry accusation and furtive gossip and to make thinking and talking about sectarianism an ordinary part of what it means to reflect on being Christian today. They have put sectarianism on the agenda as never before. In so doing, they set an example for all of us to take into the next millennium.

With the Past, in the Present, for the Future

Seán Mac Réamoinn

Introduction

The relationship between faith and culture is notoriously complex and subtle. Whether we examine it historically, or from a
sociological or even psychological viewpoint, we must take at
least three distinct but related elements into consideration: faith
itself, personal and in community; organised religion and the
church; religious culture, and its influence on the secular culture
of a society. The third of these is the main focus of this essay, but
the first two must at all times be taken into account.

Faith is of course usually born and nurtured in community –
beginning with the family: the individual believer, living his or
her faith in isolation, is a rarity. Still, in the last analysis, it is a
matter of private personal commitment, and its depth and extent can be measured, if at all, only indirectly. But such indirect
evidence as may be available, from the past as in our own time,
may be of positive value in assessing the quality of religious culture. Organised religion is, by contrast, an essentially public af-
fair, and the church as community and especially as institution,
can provide an abundance of material for analysis by the historian
and sociologist. And this in turn may help us to understand the
cultural situation.

The present, very brief, study can offer little more than a *tour
d'horizon*, and relies heavily on the work of specialist scholars,
but they are not to be held responsible for my personal observations, judgements and prejudices. For convenience I approach
the subject in three historical phases: AD 500-1560; 1560-1900;
1900-2000, with some assessment of developments at home, and
of their outward thrust. I should perhaps add that while I write

with high regard for my fellow citizens of other traditions, my reading of the story is that of an Irish Roman Catholic – *ich kann nicht anders.*

I. THE FIRST THOUSAND YEARS

I doubt if anyone will seriously disagree if I describe St Patrick's *apologia*, known as his 'Confession', as the foundation document of Irish Christianity: its authorship and authenticity are universally acknowledged. Scholars may yet have more to tell us about its dating and provenance (and of those of its companion 'Letter against Ceredic') and perhaps discover much more about its historical context, involving missionary areas and patterns in the Ireland of fifteen hundred years ago. But we can, with some conviction, repeat the words of the ancient martyrology: *Padraig uasal, aspal inse Éireann agus ceann creidimh na nGael* – 'Noble Patrick, apostle of the island of Ireland, and head of the faith of the Gaeil.'

He was not alone in bringing the good news to the people who lived on this north-western tip of the then known world, but his is the name still remembered and celebrated here, and throughout the Irish *diaspora*. The remembering may often be cloudy and distorted, and the celebration somewhat inappropriate (green beer on Broadway, drum majorettes in O'Connell Street), but that it continues to happen is the impressive thing.

What has it all to do with faith and culture? To be frank, I'm not sure. But, in some odd way, it is a kind of key, opening a gate to that People's Park we call *tradition*. And while many if not all the flowers are gone, with most of the great trees cut down, and there are an awful lot of weeds – still, not every year, but often enough, there's a new spring sowing. And the process has been going on for a long time.

As to the extent and value of the harvests, any judgement must be partial. We can only try – and of course it gets easier, if not necessarily clearer, as we move forward. The first years, however brightly lit by legend, are the darkest and most difficult.

Difficult, I mean, for us to penetrate. The gospel-bearers

themselves appear not to have had it too hard, in comparison with what we know of some similar missions elsewhere. Patrick had his own problems, as his writings make all too clear, but they were in a sense accidental: he was accused, apparently, of exceeding his brief by attempting to evangelise the wild Irish – he should have confined his ministry to those Christian settlers on the east coast. That he succeeded may have pleased God but not, at first anyway, his elders and betters across the water, who had scant regard for their Gaelic cousins.

There was, in fact, a sort of cousinship, though hardly recognised on either side, between our British Celtic neighbours and our ancestors, whom they called *Gwyddyl* – wild forest-folk (down out of the trees, but only just). The nickname stuck, by the way: we use the forms *Gaedhil* and *Gaeil!* Patrick had of course visited us long before, in uncomfortable circumstances, and wasn't afraid to come back. And I would suggest that our remote cultural kinship was of some vital support to the British missionaries, in that, however superficially Romanised many of them were, they must have recognised a way of life, a culture, not so different from what they were used to – at least outside the imperial *oppida*, already in decline.

It has always been the custom of the more sensible evangelists to accept, or at least avoid confrontation with, those 'pagan' features of life which were not plainly unacceptable. This policy seems to have worked particularly well here, and would have been made easier by that sense of kinship, or at least familiarity, which I have postulated. What was clearly of the devil was cast out; the rest was 'christened'.

I must, I suppose, plead (a little) guilty to oversimplification. But, as far as we can tell, the baptising of pagan Ireland was achieved without violence or bloodshed: there are no records of martyrdom until much later. To argue from silence is always dangerous, and there may have been occasions when the ultimate witness was called for, and given; but one would have expected the first and second generations of Christians to have cherished the names and memories of those who gave it, and to insist on their being remembered and honoured. Such does not seem to have happened. There were undoubtedly disaffected elements among those professional men of religion and learning who combined the arts of the *file* with the ministry of the *draí*. But in general, a close, even symbiotic, relationship between the new order and what the Italians call *la vecchia religione* might be seen to have been established, and to have long persisted, leaving traces into our own time.

Here one needs to proceed with caution. A remarkably easy mutual accommodation was certainly achieved early on between the new culture and that of the Celtic society in which it was planted, and this relationship was maintained in most areas of society for a very long time, surviving colonisation (in its various stages), as well as later negative attitudes on the part of the church authority – though this factor was finally instrumental in breaking the old fabric, as we shall see. The matter of mores, among a highly class-structured people, is more problematic. Religious observance must have, at least on a popular level, included some rites and customs from the pre-Christian past – sanitised, perhaps, and exorcised – judging by their long survival. But I doubt the existence of any widespread syncretism, in faith or liturgy.

Patrick himself lays down the line. In the old religion, here as among the wide range of peoples belonging to the Indoeuropean family, the worship of the sun had a certain centrality. But he proclaims that while, one day, we who die, or are put to death,

> will rise again in the brightness of the sun, that is, in the glory of Christ the Redeemer ... and will then reign from Him and through Him and in Him ... it is *at His command* that the sun rises daily as we see, and it will never have command, nor will its splendour live forever. *And all those who adore the sun will be made sadly to suffer*. We however worship the true Sun, Christ, who will never perish, *as nor will we who do His will* ...

Once that was accepted as absolute, the rest, being relative, could be accommodated. The tutelary *numina* of Loch Derg and the Mayo Reek could be 'converted': in due time, Patrick would take their place, their pilgrim cult purged, and made channels of grace for generations. What is more, the first of these, Patrick's Purgatory, as it came to be called, drew pilgrims from far away, as it 'filled Europe with its mighty rumour'. And there were a thousand other shrines: islands, and holy wells and high summer places – sacred to the old gods, now named for their Christian counterparts who inherited their guardianship. Each of these had its own *dúchas*, its own sense of belonging, and all together formed a network of devotion, a kind of catholicity of faith and experience.

A wider and more formal catholicity was of course reflected in the organisational structure (based on the imperial pattern) of which the *diocese* was the unit: Patrick himself, with the somewhat shadowy Palladius and others, were the first bishops. But within a very few generations a new pattern emerged in which the 'local church' was the *monastery*, under the rule of an abbot. And, with a few exceptions, the abbot was not in episcopal orders: bishops were subsidiary functionaries, ordained for certain sacramental duties.

And so there evolved a new network of independent but inter-related foundations, often with strong ties of kinship. Clearly, such a system could transcend boundaries of 'church' and 'society', and in fact the monasteries became centres of ordinary life and work, embryonic 'villages' and 'towns' in what was an altogether 'rural' landscape. A latter-day scholar of the subject, the late Tomás Ó Fiaich – who could himself claim the title *comharba* or successor of Patrick, as Primate of Armagh – warns us not to picture these monasteries like one of the great medieval foundations on the continent. 'It was much closer in appearance to the monastic settlements of the Nile Valley … than to later Monte Cassino or Clairvaux.'[1] The monks lived in individual *cealla* or cells, grouped around a simple oratory and other communal buildings. Craftsmen worked and lived with their families close-by, with land-holders and farmers on the perimeter.

The Irish monasteries of the sixth or seventh century, then, were not greatly imposing in appearance. Yet this was the milieu that produced that most remarkable spiritual, intellectual and artistic movement of Dark Age Europe, the 'Celtic Church'. It was also the milieu, the nursery, the laboratory, where a written Irish literature first came into being, and where an immemorial Celtic culture was saved from oblivion, and restored to that European civilisation of which it was a formative force. This all happened in the still centre of monastic learning, the *scriptorium*.

For, though Latin was the working-language of the monastic scribes as they set to the copying and illumination of scriptural and liturgical texts, they were Gaelic in speech and tradition. Their minds and hearts and memories, however dedicated to prayer and gospel, must have had room for some of the vast oral lore of *scéalaíocht* and *seanchas* and *dinnseanchas* and *filíocht* which were the matter of that tradition. And so, it was inevitable that the Latin alphabet should be adopted to the recording of this extraordinary heritage. But the monks did more: as well as recording, they edited and collated. Sometimes they censored, for some of the material was unsuitable for pious eyes, but, on the whole, they did not distort.

Certainly, the vigour of Irish oral tradition – in native scholarship as well as in popular culture – might itself have ensured the survival of much of this material, at least until the end of the Middle Ages, but much would have been lost or eroded in form or content. The pioneering work of the *scriptoria* was crucial, particularly having regard to the cultural wreckage of the Viking years. As it was, a considerable amount of what had been preserved must have been lost at the time. But enough remains to provide Ireland and Europe with at least a partial retrospective of the first Celtic millennium, with its gods and lovers and fighting men.

The eighth century saw two developments in the life and culture of monastic Ireland, one very positive, the other fatally negative. The first was that movement of spiritual and institutional reform associated with the *Céilí Dé* or 'culdees', originally in the monasteries in Tallaght and Finglas, but later more widely in Ireland, and marginally in Britain. It was a reaction against a perhaps inevitable decline in observance and practice within the peculiarities of the Irish monastic system. Certainly it succeeded on the ascetic and disciplinary level, but it also marked a new flowering of that creativity – in metal-work, in the illumination of manuscripts, in poetry – which was already characteristic of the monastic culture. The personal sensitivity of the poems which have survived is of special interest, not least when a simple delight in the natural world – of a kind later called 'Franciscan' – is expressed in a sophisticated language and metric, borrowed, or inherited, from the professional poet caste.

Unfortunately, by the end of the century, the Viking raids had begun – this was the second negative development. Both Finglas and Tallaght were only among the first to fall, among our great centres of faith and culture. It was the beginning of the end of what is not improperly called a 'golden age'. But on the other hand, both the culdee movement and the Viking depredations were, in their very different ways, potent factors in quickening the pace of Irish missionary outreach to continental Europe. This outreach may without exaggeration be claimed to have played a vital role in the preservation and renewal of both faith and culture in the West. In the re-making of Europe, Columbanus stands beside Benedict.

It would be far beyond the scope of this essay to trace, even in outline, the successive stages of the continental mission: from the first contacts with Celtic Brittany, to the age of Columbanus and his associates (beginning in the last decade of the sixth century); by way of Fiachra, Cilian, Fursa, down to Sedulius and Eriugena and Feargal the astronomer; and, finally, the *Schotten-klöster* (12th century) which, as Tomás Ó Fiaich points out, gave Ireland 'an extra bridge to Europe'. As he says:

> Henceforth the traffic was two-way. European influences poured into Ireland with the Cistercians and Augustinian Canons (and, in the next century the new mendicant orders), the institution of the Irish dioceses and parishes, the reforming synods, the appointment of Papal Legates. Irish clerics in

turn were frequently travellers to Europe – *ad limina* visits to Rome, journeys there for the pallium and the Lateran Councils. Inevitably, some Irish churchmen died on the Continent with a reputation for sanctity – Malachy in Clairvaux in 1148, Conchobhar Mac Conchoille in Chambéry in 1175, Lorcán O'Toole in Eu in 1180.[2]

In fact the 'European influences' noted by Ó Fiaich were in several cases strong forces for centralisation, as well as for reform and renewal. Irish territorial dioceses were constituted or re-constituted at the Synod of Rath Breasail (1111), Malachy became Archbishop of Armagh in 1132, his successor was acknowledged as primate twenty years later at the Synod of Kells, and 1157 saw the first Irish Cistercian foundation, Mellifont Abbey, duly consecrated. It was the end of the 'Celtic' church and the older monastic Ireland, and with the Norman barons in Bannow Bay in 1169, it might seem to have been the end of Gaelic Ireland.

But that was not (is not?) yet. The noble, if rather shaky, institutions of the older civilisation remained standing until the early seventeenth century: the Irish language and much of the traditional way of life continued to survive considerably longer – how long and how strong we will later discuss. But the fact that the colonising efforts of our neighbours stayed less than successful, to any significant degree, through the remainder of the Middle Ages, would seem to indicate that culture can be stronger and tougher and more resilient than political power. It would also appear that a culture where sacred and secular coexist on reasonably good terms, can cope effectively with such forces as would try to drive a wedge between these, even when invoking religious authority to this end.

Among Ó Fiaich's 'European influences', he notes the arrival of the 'new mendicant orders'. That happened in the thirteenth century: Franciscans and Dominicans came within a few years of their founders' deaths, and, along with the Carmelites and Augustinians, soon became part of the Irish religious scene. Like the Cistercians and the Canons Regular, they gained the patronage of the Norman settlers and were quick to establish themselves in the *towns* – Galway, New Ross, Drogheda, Kilkenny,

Clonmel and the rest – which were, as historian F. X. Martin OSA has written, 'one of the lasting Norman gifts to the country'.

But Gaelic patronage was also forthcoming, and many of the convents and priories, established under the aegis of both 'Old Irish' and Gaelicised Normans, attracted novices who were innocent of the new language and the new ways. This inevitably led to tensions and official disapproval (to put it mildly). And the fact that no fewer than nine Dominicans of Gaelic affiliation had been ordained as bishops before the end of the thirteenth century (that is within eight years of the Order's arrival here) – including two archbishops (of Armagh and of Cashel) – shows how the wind was blowing. And these were all counted as members of the Irish Vicariate of the English Province! Needless to say, there were thunderous denunciations from high places, with allegations of treason and disaffection. Even Pope John XXII was made to utter solemn threats of excommunication (in 1317). But the Gaelic brethren remained unimpressed.

On a more positive note, the contribution of the friars (principally that of the Franciscans and Dominicans) to medieval Gaelic literature was very substantial, as was their provision of Irish versions of liturgical, philosophical and devotional texts. All this literary activity, which renewed the old close traditional relationship between religious community and traditional culture, took place against a backdrop of Gaelic socio-political resurgence. Whatever the shortcomings, in planning or strategy, of those who hoped to see an end to the Norman-English settlement, there can be no doubting the vigour of their culture, or of its capacity to unite and enrich the lives of those who, whatever their origin, found in it a viable common ground.

It should also be noted that the reformist and 'observantine' movements or 'tendencies' among the friars in the fourteenth and fifteenth centuries appear to have been at their strongest in the Gaelic foundations: those currents, by the way, were not alone of disciplinary import, they were rooted in a recognition of the need for spiritual renewal. This renewal was to stand both friars and people in good stead at the Reformation.

The Wars of the Roses and other conflicts in high places, as well as the ongoing hostilities between the Pale administration and the turbulent Earls (and their Gaelic allies), were reflected in divisions in the hierarchical Irish church. Even church buildings became the victims of neglect by those in whose care they had been placed. At the beginning of the fifteenth century, a report on the state of religion declares:

> For there is no archbishop, no bishop, abbot nor prior, person nor vicar, nor any other person of the church, high or low, great or small, English or Irish, that is accustomed to preach the word of God, saving the poor friar beggars ...

Even allowing for exaggeration, one can see that were it not for the friars 'Catholic Ireland' would have been ill-prepared for the Reformation and its aftermath. We have alas! no direct record or evidence of what the *laos* felt or thought, or believed, or how they prayed: no 15th or 16th century predecessor of the 'Religious Songs of Connacht'. But we can say with some confidence that the more sophisticated laity, as represented by the *filí*, were often men of authentic faith: this becomes clear on the rare occasions when personal feeling and vision comes through the classic objectivity of their verse. (This is constant through the high Middle Ages.) And for the rest: well, there remained Loch Derg, and the Reek and all those holy wells ...

II. FROM REFORMATION TO EMANCIPATION

This period of four centuries (give or take a decade or two) is the one in which Irish faith and culture were made to prove their durability in spite of, not just 'dungeon, fire and sword', but also the slow erosion of basic rights and ordinary decencies, not to mention most of the small comforts of life and the graciousness of common civility. By faith, I mean, for the greater part, that corpus of belief and observance which was the inheritance of the vast majority of the people born into and raised in the Roman Catholic tradition. The arrival and growth of other traditions I acknowledge and salute; I do not doubt their authenticity. But, historically, they belong, directly or indirectly, to the process of colonisation; indeed, it can and must be said that without the impetus of 16th-century religious ideology, the English colonial adventure could hardly have been as successful as it was, here or elsewhere

For nearly two hundred years, from Henry VIII's initial legislation to the enactment and implementation of the notorious Penal Laws, the twin forces of Protestant militancy and colonial aggression set to destroy or at least to transform Irish society. And, armed with the highly efficient weapon of 'plantation', they met with a considerable measure of success, notably in the area known today as Northern Ireland. Elsewhere, colonisation did very well in the administration of power – for a very long time. But I anticipate. For the moment it is sufficient to say that successive Tudor, Jacobite, Cromwellian and Williamite campaigns finally destroyed what there was of an Irish *polity*, and did very considerable damage to the *structures* of Gaelic culture, and of the Roman Catholic religion.

But both faith and culture appear to have survived, in however broken or diminished a form. There were, of course, individual episodes of appalling savagery, and the Cromwellian years in particular do seem to have earned the heritage of horror which they engendered: revisionism can do little there. But of course, *a scéal féin scéal gach éinne*, and the Ulster Rising of 1641 has left its own dark legends.

War, its attendant savageries and miseries, is however not the only destroyer of a civilisation. The disintegration of Gaelic society in the seventeenth century was chronicled, painfully and with a burning anger, by Dáibhí Ó Bruadair – who incidentally in an early poem, *Adoramus Te Christe*, wrote the marvellous lines:

mar ghréin tré ghloin do léimeadh sibh d'aonscrios oilc Ádhaimh,
go rugais le crann duine 's a chlann a hifearn ceann Cásca ...

you made a leap like sun through glass to abolish Adam's evil
and saved with a cross Man and his tribe at Eastertime from Hell
(version: Michael Hartnett[3])

Ó Bruadair was a professional poet, trained in the best of

schools; of remote Norse ancestry, his great patrons were Hiberno-Norman, the Fitzgeralds and the Burkes. But, by the 17th century, all that was subsumed into the Gaelic *ethos*. The process of being 'beaten into clay' (Yeats) was well under way:

> *Our priests are scarred with greed and pride*
> *and all our poets are cut down to size*
> *but, worst of all, I realise*
> *that no one poor is considered wise ...*

(version: Michael Hartnett)

Ó Bruadair survived the defeats of the Boyne and Limerick, but he was not at ease in the new society. He and his kind were not humble men: they knew their place and it was a high one. The democratic idea had not yet been born. But though the social framework within which the old culture had flourished was destroyed forever, the culture itself, and the language and literary energy which were at its heart, lived on. As Michael Hartnett has written:

> The eighteenth century was perhaps the most active time ever known for the production of poetry; but it was the people, rather than the professional poets, who began to sing – the poetry came out of cabins rather than castles. Ó Bruadair would have hated it ...

Gaelic scholarship and the cultivation of a 'high' literature did not of course disappear with the defeat of Kinsale, or the Flight of the Earls, or the depredations of Cromwell. Ó Bruadair was not the only one to illuminate the darkening seventeenth-century landscape: the names of Geoffrey Keating, Piaras Feirtéar, Pádraigín Haicéad OP, Ruaidhrí Ó Flaithbheartaigh, an Dubhal-tach Mac Firbhisigh, Mícheál Ó Cleirigh OFM and his collabor-ators in the 'Annals of the Four Masters' – these and others attest to the enormous activity of the *fir léinn* of the time, as well as to the creative energy of the poets among them. And the list includes, as any such record must, friars and other men in holy orders. While much of their work was done in Ireland, a significant part of it was carried out in what was generally the more secure and peaceful milieu of Irish houses of study abroad – in Belgium,

France, Rome, Bohemia and elsewhere; most notably in the Franciscan colleges at Louvain (Leuven) and Prague.

It was in the Low Countries that the first printed book in Gaelic was published under Catholic auspices (in Antwerp in 1611). This was the first in a stream of publications whose significance for the survival and development of Irish Catholicism can only be surmised. Some of the great Franciscan names associated with the project included Aodh MacAingil, later appointed Archbishop of Armagh, Bonaventura Ó hEodhusa, Antaine Gearnon, Theobald Stapleton (Galduf) and Pilib Ó Raghallaigh (in Prague).

The direct influence of the Louvain school was substantial, but it was only one very important part of a pattern of Irish-continental exchange which preserved Irish religion and Irish culture from lapsing into a backwater. It may be particularly worth noting that the initial stages of this Irish outreach coincided with the Counter-Reformation and the age of the Baroque. The implications of this for both Irish Catholicism and Irish religious writings (including Keating, as well as the Louvain school) has perhaps been overlooked until recently. I would refer the interested reader to the pioneering work of Dr Tadhg Ó Dúshláine of NUI, Maynooth – notably, his monograph, *An Eoraip agus Litríocht na Gaeilge 1600-1650* (Clóchomhar). Another post-Reformation strengthening of the European linkage came with the arrival of the Jesuits, as well as the enlargement of the Franciscan and Carmelite families (Capuchins and Discalced friars respectively).

Circumstances dictated the European linkage forged by the continuing exodus of young men to continental seminaries in the seventeenth and eighteenth centuries. It was of course matched by the more secular emigration of aspiring medics, lawyers, military professionals – not forgetting the wine trade. But it would seem that few of these retained the same consciousness of their cultural identity as did the friars.

It would be churlish at this point not to mention the name of that picaresque figure, Tomás MacCasaide, sometime friar of the Augustinian community of Ballyhaunis in Mayo. He is not the only Augustinian to make a significant contribution to Gaelic literature – one thinks of Liam Inglis (1709-1778), priest, poet and student of international politics. But 'An Casaideach Bán', as he is remembered, was, as they say, something else. A near contemporary of Inglis, he served as a trooper in the guard of Frederick the Great of Prussia and acquired a high reputation as an amiable rogue. He was a worthy successor to some of the more colourful figures who made a brief appearance in Helen Waddell's marvellous classic *The Wandering Scholars*.

The Irish eighteenth century was a time when Irish fortunes might be seen to be at their lowest ebb. The period of the Penal Laws was indeed one of the darkest in our history. The severity and inhumanity of the code were successful in reducing the native population to a position of poverty and impotence. The 'Protestant Nation' was firmly established – *in perpetuum* it seemed. The ministers of the people's church were hounded and persecuted (though not as uniformly as reputed: inefficiency and even human decency did, from time to time, break in). But it was all in the cause of political and economic power: attempts to 'convert' the papists were sporadic, half-hearted and bedevilled by differences of policy on the use of the Irish language as a means of instruction and evangelisation.

This eighteenth century and its laws brought great misery to the poorest people, but, as ever, there were times and places when things were easier. And there was always that network of religious tradition, with its patron days ('patterns'), and *turais* to holy wells, and occasions like *Lúnasa*, and St Brigid's Eve, and May eve, and Midsummer: there was music and song and dancing. The old culture survived, and the people survived with it.

This survival was not confined to rural Ireland. Although the towns and cities remained strongholds of Anglicisation, most if not all maintained Irish-speaking populations of varying sizes, including servants, labourers, small traders and the like, often concentrated in Gaelic ghettos or 'Irishtowns'. Dublin was no exception. Already at the beginning of the seventeenth century, we read of some of the city's first Jesuits 'working among the Gaelic-speaking poor'. And a century and a half later, an ac-

count of the Sunday timetable of the Dominican Chapel in
Bridge Street (dated 1761) refers to the 'most useful and necessary sermon' as that preached in Irish at 7 a.m. for the benefit of
'those who know no English'. And there continued to be many
such for another hundred years and more, especially as long as
the capital's immediate hinterland was largely Irish-speaking.

There were (as there still are) Gaelic immigrants from farther
afield. Two of the most celebrated were Roscommon-born Seán
Ó Neachtain and his son Tadhg who were at the centre of a literary circle whose names are recorded in a poem dated 1728. The
group, which included three priests and one medical doctor,
were from all the four Provinces, but mostly from Leinster.

Later in the century, interest in the Irish language and Irish
music developed among a generation of young radical intellectuals in Belfast. This brought recognition that the national culture
could be shared by men and women of different traditions and
religious subscription, pointing to what could be a fruitful alliance of 'Protestant, Catholic and Dissenter'.

The last part of the century brought Catholic relief, although
it did not affect the poorest or next-to-poorest (the *cosmhuintir*)
very much. Rather, the potato was that magical gift which en-
abled them to increase and multiply. And as they multiplied,
and as the better off among them made their way in trade, slowly
the Catholic nation found its feet.

And there were new and dangerous ideas abroad. The Rights
of Man, and *talamh gan chíos* … and 'Pastorini'. There was the
Rising of '98, and its aftermath … rights and rent-free land would
have to wait a while. But what 'Pastorini,' alias Bishop Charles
Walmsley, had to say was a different matter: he forecast the final
victory of Catholicism in 1825, as was to be seen in St John's
gospel – *an té a thuigfeadh é*. His apocalyptic teachings were received with enthusiasm by poets like Raifteirí and Mangan, and
by a considerable sector of rural Catholic Ireland. Pastorini was,
oddly enough, a Fellow of the Royal Society, distinguished as a
mathematical astronomer. And, after all, he was only four years
out on the date of Emancipation …

III. CATHOLIC IRELAND

'You'll be still breaking stones!' This was allegedly Daniel O'Connell's answer to the day-labourer who asked what *he* would get from Emancipation. It sounds apocryphal: the Liberator wasn't much given to that kind of realism. In fact Emancipation meant very little to the majority of the plain people, least of all to those at or near the bottom of the pile. And it was they who increased so outrageously in number, in a population explosion which filled the island of Ireland with eight million souls and bodies (and mouths) by 1841. Within a few years a million had died of starvation or disease. Another million got away. It's called the Great Famine, but by those whose memories were closest, *an drochshaol* – 'the bad times'. It was the first of four seismic events which changed Irish society in the nineteenth century.

In the welter of ritual lamentation, serious assessment and silly revisionism, which marked the century-and-a-half commemoration a couple of years ago, one public remark rang out clear as a bell. It was made by Luke Dodd, then of the Famine Museum in Roscommon: 'Let us always remember,' he said, 'that the Famine was *class specific.*'

It is a fact we tend to forget, and in forgetting it, we are liable to distort the whole situation in rural Ireland, then and in the years which followed. The received wisdom seems to be that the Famine hit us all (or, rather, all our ancestors) – with the exception of those ruffianly landlords. We ignore the inherent class structure of our society and that, while the personnel of the categories may change, still the fact of a structure differentiation by levels of power, wealth and influence remains.

Put crudely, in post-Famine Ireland, the class-structure was thinned out from the bottom. The lowest quarter was wiped out, while another fraction lurked uneasily on the margins. Some of these died within a few years; others went into internal exile, in the anonymous slums then building up in Dublin and elsewhere. Yet others took to the roads, making common cause –

when permitted – with itinerant craftsmen and their families, to form a new 'travelling community', still with us. There were indeed individual victims of famine fever from several social strata: priests, ministers, religious sisters, volunteer workers of all religious traditions and of none, as well as accidental casualties of infection. But the great mass of those who died or were 'displaced' were the poorest of the poor.

To describe a church synod as 'seismic' might seem more than a little exaggerated, but the programme of reform and re-organisation introduced by the Synod of Thurles (1850) under the formidable Paul Cardinal Cullen did result in a sort of social earthquake: this might not have happened were it not for a third development or process which, coming to a head at that time, provided the synod with a congenial context for the enforcement and acceptance of new rules and new mores. I refer to the abandonment of the Irish language by the majority of people as a common vernacular. In tandem, Cullen's 'Devotional Revolution' and the rejection of the ancestral language, with its immemorial store of inherited values and *pietas*, brought about a change in culture (including, and perhaps especially, religious culture) more radical than had ever been achieved by colonial or penal legislation.

Of course, the process had begun long before. The condemnation of 'abuses' in popular religious practice was an old strain in episcopal pronouncements: as I recall, the Synod of Jamestown, at the very beginning of the seventeenth century, was preoccupied with *inter alia* the pagan rite of *libation* at funerals! (Funerals and weddings were of course notoriously 'dangerous occasions' ... was the problem really 'abuses' or the threat of a rival liturgy?) And, as to the adoption of English by the common people, the process moved forward, as and when prospects of advancement – to which English was seen to be the key – improved. It began (apart from the towns) in the second half of the eighteenth century and continued well into our time. The tragedy was that it seemed to be an article of faith that to learn to speak English you must abandon Irish. It was a simple case of 'either ... or'.

And so there came the monstrous conspiracy of school and home with its cruel 'tally-rod' weaponry which, later, supported by continental pietisms and Victorian mores, went a long way to destroying a people's culture, a way of life, a people's memory. And the sad irony is that it was all well-intentioned: all for the good of God's people and, domestically, for the 'children's future'.

The consequent tragedy, personal and communal, is uniquely expressed in these lines from John Montague's poem, *A Grafted Tongue*:

> An Irish
> child weeps in school
> repeating its English.
> After each mistake
>
> The master
> gouges another mark
> on the tally stick
> hung around its neck
>
> Like a bell
> on a cow, a hobble
> on a straying goat.
> To slur and stumble
>
> In shame
> the altered syllables
> of your own name;
> to stray sadly home
>
> And find
> the turf-cured width
> of your parent's hearth
> growing slowly alien:
>
> In cabin
> and field, they still
> speak the old tongue.
> You may greet no one.

To grow
a second tongue, as
harsh a humiliation
as twice to be born.

The fourth event which changed Ireland in the nineteenth century was the successful struggle for land ownership which, establishing a rural society based largely on peasant proprietorship, brought about a *petit bourgeois* revolution, setting the social foundation for a new Irish polity. Home Rule when it came would develop on solid conservative-agrarian lines with the blessing of the majority church. Marginal elements in society, of whom the most numerous would probably be agricultural labourers, would find their place in this pattern. On the other hand, the remaining larger landowners and the Protestant minority in general would be guaranteed their liberties without discrimination, within what would be an overwhelmingly 'Catholic ethos' – an ethos strengthened and deepened from new continental sources, through the mission and pastoral work of the Vincentians, Passionists, Redemptorists and Marists. Nor must we forget the pioneering and often heroic labours of religious sisters and brothers in the teaching and nursing fields.

That things did not work out quite as envisaged was due to the emergence of unforeseen social and cultural ideas in the last years of the century. The Gaelic revival came just in time to preserve something of what might have been completely lost, and also to inspire new possibilities, new ways forward. The tradition of political revolution which looked back to 1798, but might appear to have ended with the apparent fiasco of the Fenian rising, was still alive. The pike still in the rafters, even if it had gone a bit rusty. 'Foreign' ideas of socialism and social democracy were gaining currency. And here and there the *sean-nós* still survived, in religious belief as in song!

It must be emphasised, however, that the whole post-Famine picture is two-dimensional. There is the island of Ireland with its people: and there is the *diaspora*. It is no longer a matter of links – ecclesial, cultural, professional – with continental Europe, long-established and significant though many of these were. The Irish presence in America, as in England, Scotland, Wales and in the 'new' British colonies, rapidly achieved a considerable import-ance in numbers, and later in influence.

The importance of Irish immigration as a dominant factor in the growth of Roman Catholicism in these countries hardly needs stressing. Sadly, however, occurring as it did at a time when traditional culture was becoming etiolated and underval-ued, it failed to contribute a distinctive dimension to the new re-ligious cultures. If Irish usually meant Catholic, it also meant English in language. An age-old faith had to wear borrowed dress, and express itself in second-hand sentimentalities.

None of this takes from the great support and solidarity given by the emigrés and their children to Irish aspirations, political but also cultural. Most of this support was moral and financial, and very valuable it was. The intellectual, academic and creative contribution would come much later.

IV. IRISH IRELAND

If we accept P. H. Pearse's dictum that 'when the Gaelic League was founded (1893) the Irish Revolution began', then the Revolution was a sturdy infant in the early years of the new century, and had matured to full manhood – and womanhood– by 1916. Douglas Hyde's movement of rediscovery and renewal had allies who, at least partially, shared his vision and that of Eoin MacNéill. It was given political and social flesh in Griffith's Sinn Féin; in Connolly's socialism and Larkin's trade unionism; in the cooperative movement; in the IRB and the GAA – these last two being more closely linked than might appear. And Cumann na mBan came to recruit the more militantly minded among those women who were enthusiastic members of the Gaelic League.

The fact that Hyde was the son of a country parson was obvi-ously no small guarantee that the League was, as it claimed to be, 'non-political and non-sectarian'. In the early years it attracted a membership of diverse religious and political traditions from all over the country. Indeed it seemed that the language might in time become a bond uniting all classes and creeds, north and south, as some of the Belfast radicals had hoped over a hundred years earlier.

It was not to be: by 1915 the League had committed itself to political nationalism, and all but a minority of Protestants, north and south, left the movement. That minority, however, and their successors were to contribute much to national culture and political life. And Hyde's own personal contribution was to be belatedly recognised when, by general agreement, he became first President of Ireland under the 1937 Constitution.

Still, the label 'Gaelic, Catholic, Nationalist' continues to be used in order to sum up the dominant strain in Irish society over most of this century. The three elements were certainly present in the culture in which the political and social changes leading to independence were rooted and which have informed our society until recently. But linked though they were seen to have been, and often were, the three must be recognised as distinct and discrete.

In the early years of the century 'nationalism' was a concept to which almost all Irish Catholics would subscribe. It was sufficiently inclusive to embrace everybody from post-Parnellite home rulers to hard-line physical force 'Fenians'. Not that the latter, or for that matter supporters of Sinn Féin, were enamoured of the word: they would regard it as too 'soft' (in contrast to those of a later generation to whom it carries overtones of Fascism!).

As to the 'Gaelic' element, while the vision of the revival was enormously influential, across a wide range of 'national' bodies dedicated to social and political renewal, each maintained its own ethos and ideology, serving its particular interests and objectives. The 'Gaelic' influence remained, in many cases, more a matter of symbol than of practical action. Only a minority actually learned the language or used it in their various activities.

One of the most striking ways in which Douglas Hyde's own work helped to shape a new Irish culture was, ironically, through his English translations of the verse material he collected from among the Irish-speaking people of Connacht. The beauty and intensity of the *Amhráin Ghrá* (Love Songs) effectively served to change the course of Irish verse in the English language.

The same was true, if perhaps to a lesser extent, of the *Amhráin Diadha* (Religious Songs). But the great significance of the publication of these verses was the unveiling of one part of a heritage of traditional spirituality which had been hidden from most Irish people for anything from fifty to a hundred years. It re-opened doors of perception to those, priest and people, who cared enough to enter. But, institutionally, it left the church untouched. Gestures of goodwill, the recitation of a decade of the rosary in Irish, an Irish sermon on St Patrick's Day – this was about the sum of 'official' Catholic involvement in a restoration of Gaelic culture. And when a remarkable popular coalition forced the new National University to make Irish an essential subject for matriculation, this happened in the teeth of strong opposition from the Catholic bishops!

Still, the popular (populist?) culture of 'Irish Ireland', as D. P. Moran of the *Leader*, one of its most trenchant promoters, called it, did appear to take for granted that it was co-terminous with 'Catholic Ireland' (with a number of honoured if eccentric exceptions). And since those of an older generation who were loyal to the Home Rule tradition were equally loyal to the church – with the exception of some unrepentant Parnellites – one can readily understand how the still dominant religious element in our culture left little need or room for dissent. (And in fact there seems to have been a high degree of religious observance among the new radical leaders – however suspicious some church authorities might be of their politics.) So, if to those of another culture, Home Rule had meant Rome Rule, later, more extreme nationalist aspirations did not appear to offer any more palatable alternatives.

This was of no trivial import. As I have suggested earlier, Reformation religious ideology was a powerful dynamic in the English colonial adventure which brought about the Plantation

of Ulster, and continued to motivate the social and political culture of unionism for four hundred years. So, when 'Gaelic,
Catholic, Nationalist' Ireland seemed to offer a real threat to
their way of life, the loyalists' response came strong and clear.
On September 28th 1912, a 'day of dedication' was marked
throughout Ulster by Protestant religious services and the sign-
ing of a Solemn League and Covenant. Nearly a quarter of a million men pledged to use 'all means which may be found necessary to defeat the present conspiracy to set up a Home Rule
Parliament in Ireland'. This was followed by the enrollment of
an Ulster Volunteer Force, and arms were brought in from
Germany.

One sector of the cultural landscape, north and south, did
however remain unaffected by religious affiliation, not to say
orthodoxy. The founding fathers of the new literature in English
– whether of Anglo-Irish Protestant background: Yeats, Synge,
AE; or 'cradle Catholics': Joyce, Moore – remained aloof from
the prevailing 'faith and fatherland' duality. (Although Joyce's
work is permeated by Catholic belief and thought.) They, and
many of their successors were, and too long continued to be, regarded with suspicion, even hostility, by the populist mainstream – often with encouragement from high places.

And yet it was Yeats, the aristocrat, who told the groundlings
that they had 'disgraced themselves again'. It was he who, when
'Irish Ireland' transcended itself in the 1916 Rising, saw that
thenceforth, *all was changed, changed utterly…*' Following the ex-
ecution of the leaders and the immediate aftermath of something like despair, there came a quickening of new hope, a
recognition of new possibilities, which expressed itself unam-
biguously in the 1918 Election.

V. NATION AND STATE

I now declare an interest. As one of the first generation to grow
up in an independent Irish State I propose to write of the last
seventy years principally from memory – a notoriously unreli-

able method, but at least a bit different. I begin in 1929. That was the year we celebrated the centenary of Emancipation, and I was one of a multitude of children at a Mass in Phoenix Park.

Three years later, I was at another Childrens' Mass in the Park, during the Eucharistic Congress. This was an international event, the first of its kind – civil or religious – to be held in an independent Ireland. Even a ten-year-old could recognise the scale and size of it, and enjoy something of the pomp and ceremony: nor was I too young to relish the reported remark of the 'oul wan' when she saw the Monstrance carried under a canopy, borne on the one side by President de Valera and, on the other, by ex-President Cosgrave, 'Sure it isn't the first time He was between two thieves!'

My political education developed when we moved to Clonmel which was one of the areas where Dev's men and the Blueshirts joined in conflict (peacefully, on the whole). Culturally, as a Mass-server in the Franciscan Friary, I was exposed for the first time to Palestrina and Vittoria, and, in general, to an awareness of continental Europe. And in the Christian Brothers' High School I developed a taste for the Irish Language – which was still spoken close to the town, though I was hardly aware of this.

My 'taste' deepened into something more serious when we moved again, this time to Galway, where I was a pupil at Coláiste Iognáid (run by the Jesuits), and afterwards a student in University College. In both cases, I was fortunate in my mentors, and finally emerged reasonably unscarred, and without any deep resentment of authority.

I am conscious that I seem to have lapsed into autobiography, which is not what I am about. I am also conscious that I only gradually became aware of the deep flaws and wounds in our society, of widespread poverty and social injustice, of the inadequacies in our educational system, of the authoritarianism of the church to which I belonged. Galway is a city of many parishes and religious orders, so religious observance was pervasive, but not uniform, and certainly not oppressive. Names like Letterfrack or Magdalen Laundry bore no sinister overtones.

One was aware of Mussolini's oppression in Ethiopia, and later of the Spanish Civil War – on which popular opinion was by no means uniform. A lot depended on whether you read the *Independent* or the *Press*. The latter followed the de Valera line of non-involvement, and many who were no great admirers of the 'Long Fellow' in domestic affairs, respected his international stature in the League of Nations. 'O'Duffy's Brigade' of pro-Franco volunteers were not universally seen as fighters for the faith, nor were the Irish members of the International Brigade all condemned as red villains.

Much has been written about the 'Emergency' of 1939 to 1945, and of Irish neutrality in the Second World War. To suggest that this was an invention of de Valera, 'imposed' on a reluctant population, is utter nonsense, as anyone who lived through those years would agree. In de Valera's celebrated radio reply to Churchill's speech taunting Ireland at the War's end (1945) he spoke for the nation. I heard the broadcast in a Dublin café in which most of the tables were occupied by clergy of the Church of Ireland – it was Synod week, so those present came from all over Ireland. His words were heard in dead silence which lasted a full half-minute after he had finished. And then – applause such as I have rarely heard.

Economically, the Emergency years were at best a time of 'frugal comfort', that well-intentioned but unfortunate phrase, redolent of 'Catholic Social Teaching'. It would have been much worse for many but for that leak in our neutrality which allowed (forced) us to export many of our young men and women to work in Britain's munitions factories and other centres of 'full employment'. (As well as some thousands who fought in her armed forces.) And when the war was over, this emigration continued and increased, notably in the nineteen-fifties, when the Republic (declared in 1949) seemed to have despaired of ever supporting its modest population. A sign of the times was the growing concern of the Irish church for the welfare of emigrants: this included 'missions' conducted in Irish in certain cross-channel urban centres which had become off-shore *Gaeltachtaí*.

Social concern was also evident at home in the Muintir na Tíre rural life movement led by the redoubtable Fr John Hayes, and in Catholic 'Social Weeks' and other social gatherings inspired by the Papal Encyclical *Quadragesimo Anno* (1941). For some of us in the nineteen-forties, it might appear that we were being shown a 'third way' between capitalism and socialism. But I think it not unfair to say that, in the long run, all that remained of that Christian idealism in practice was an obsessive fear of state 'interference' in social, educational and medical matters, culminating in the 'Mother and Child' fiasco of 1950-51. Ironically, I believe that the display of naked authoritarianism shown by the bishops' spokesmen, and the government's submission to their wishes, was the beginning of the end of the church's 'special position' in the Irish polity.

I was in a town in Mayo when the story of the confrontation broke. The degree of popular support, on all sides, for Noel Browne was extraordinary. But even more remarkable was the near unanimous criticism of the bishops, who were widely seen as 'having gone too far this time', and, perhaps even more significantly, as being 'wrong' in their judgement of the proposed scheme. More detailed criticism was to be read not alone (predictably) in the *Irish Times*, but in such unexpected quarters as the magazine *Comhar*, journal of Irish-speaking students and graduates.

Comhar had since 1942 been making a valuable contribution to national culture in another area, providing a platform for a new wave of poets including Seán Ó Ríordáin, Máire Mhac an tSaoi, Mairtín Ó Direáin and Séamus Ó Néill, whose work seemed to herald a second Gaelic spring. And rumours – justified in the event – of powerful new work in prose kept coming during the Emergency from the Curragh internment camp, where Mairtín Ó Cadhain was Master of a republican 'university'. His novel *Cré na Cille* appeared in 1948.

Undoubtedly the most influential journal of the time was *The Bell* (1940-54) edited by Seán Ó Faoláin, and later Peadar O'Donnell. Contributors ranged from Frank O'Connor to Flann

O'Brien, including poets like Austin Clarke, Patrick Kavanagh, and, from the North, W. R. Rogers and John Hewitt. Ó Faoláin as editor was trenchant in his criticism of the more simplistic readings of nationality, of culture, of educational desiderata. He was merciless in his denunciation of the crazy excesses of our 'literary' censorship, and made many of us aware for the first time of the injustices to Irish writers (and Irish readers), committed in our name. An 'Appeal Board', set up in 1946 did mitigate some of the worst effects of the Censorship Act, which had been passed in 1929 to what was general parliamentary and popular acclaim. Oddly enough, we never had a formal Theatre Censorship. (This fact provided a useful riposte to English critics of Irish puritanism!)

VI. CULTURAL REVOLUTION

'Our country is in a highly mobile phase at present … We have set in train certain great and far-reaching processes within the material culture which inevitably will have great and far-reaching effects in other dimensions of the culture, have already had such effects.'

Thus Fr Feichín Ó Dochartaigh, professor of psychology in the National University (Dublin), in an essay in *Studies* in 1963. And he expressed it even more succinctly:

In fact we are going through a deep and far-reaching cultural revolution.

(Quoted by Professor Terence Brown in his valuable *Ireland: A Social and Cultural History (1922-1979).*)

Looking back on the Ireland of 1963, one can only admire Professor Ó Dochartaigh's remarkable perceptivity in recognising what was afoot. For only a few of the great agents of change were then operative. The Second Vatican Council was barely a year old, and Irish Television its senior by only a few months.

These two very disparate entities have been very significant in the promotion of social and cultural change. It may be argued that the encyclical *Humanae Vitae* (1968) has been a far greater influence, negatively at least as much as positively, on faith and morals than all the documents of *Vatican II*. But the direct and indirect cultural effects of the council have been profound – from Sunday observance and the use of the vernacular, to Catholic-Protestant relations, to the slow awakening of a social conscience, to a decline in popular devotionalism, to the secularisation of many areas of social life.

It should be emphasised that secularisation is not to be equated with *secularism*. Secularism implies the attempted exclusion of any consideration of the transcendent, the supernatural, the divine, from human affairs. Secularisation of society, or of any part of it, need not imply such exclusion: rather does it recognise and facilitate the autonomy of a social activity, and perhaps its 'liberation' from 'religious' fosterage (however useful or even necessary this may have been in its development).

Of course, in facilitating such a process, the postconciliar church has been merely recognising currents in Irish society which were, rather later than elsewhere, brought about by other major 'agents of change': economic development initiated by the Lemass-Whittaker programme of the late 50s and 60s; the gradual shift of emphasis from rural to urban; the women's movement; reasonably inexpensive access to 'foreign' holiday travel; the decline of censorship of films and books; the availability of reasonably reliable methods of contraception. To these there may most recently be added: provision for civil divorce and remarriage, and, in the realm of communications, the rapid growth of new technologies – the internet, websites and so on.

Not all the developments on the above list may be regarded as unmixed blessings. Nor has the church of the majority come to terms with all of them, though most of its members have, for good *and* ill. Clearly, the cultural scaffolding – of habit, assent, consensus, obedience, tradition or whatever – within which Irish Catholicism flourished for a century and a half, has collapsed. A few bits and pieces remain, but not for much longer. Scaffolding commonly betokens either demolition or a new building, or both. What have we in this instance? While the removal of the scaffolding has revealed no empty space, no vacuum

... (so far?) ... no bright new church shines out. (Why should we expect either?)

Statistics must not be ignored. The figures for Sunday Mass, for 'confessions', for 'vocations', for marriages and even baptisms are hardly encouraging. As regards the first, two things must be said: for decades the figures were abnormally high for *attendance*, but who can measure *participation*? Communion among these attending is now apparently much higher than in the past. As to the 'vocations crisis', a subject too complex to deal with here, let me say that the Irish presence in what we used to call the Third World remains very significant.

What causes one most concern is the apparent trivialisation of faith, sacrament, and let me add, sexuality, among our younger *generations* (I stress the plural). One may be tempted to judge rashly on the causes or origins, but I am convinced that my own generation (and perhaps our parents') have been at least partly responsible. There has been (was?) far too much emphasis on obligations and punishments and far too little on mutuality and gift and commitment. The current decline in marriage, the common acceptability of the word 'partner', should surely make us examine our ageing consciences: if marital commitment with a sacramental dimension has become a chore rather than a happy choice, how have we presented it to our children? How have unwilling and uneasy celibates promoted it?

So we are led to the unavoidable subject of the 'scandals' which have disfigured the Irish church and damaged its teaching power – especially, for obvious reasons, on matters of sexual morality. Those appalling incidents which have to do with the abuse of children have clear implications, institutional as well as personal, and reflect on the quality of society as a whole; the more 'normal' offences must inevitably raise questions about celibacy as an *imposed* discipline.

Our immediate concern here, however, is with the way these events have contributed to the sea-change in our culture as a whole in recent decades. It would be wrong to regard them as solely responsible for the dislodgement of institutional religion as a dominant cultural force. More important, though less obvious, has been the slow but sure rejection of false 'absolutes' in values and behaviour. Unhappily, while this should have led to an enhanced affirmation of the one Absolute – as Christians would see the God of Love – it has too often meant a rejection of the centre of faith, with a consequent trivialisation of all values. And it has to be said that some, perhaps most of the blame lies with generations of bad teaching and preaching which absolutised the relative to a degree that was at once comic and tragic. (Tirades against 'late dances'; the demonising of unmarried mothers.)

One fundamental area of Christian behaviour where the church has given admirable leadership in recent years is that of social justice, articulating principles and attitudes far more radical than the more tentative approach of fifty years ago. As far back as 1972 the bishops' pastoral *The Work of Justice* proclaimed:

> There is no such thing in justice … as an absolute right to do what I like with my money, my profits, my capital, my property, my land … It is morally unacceptable to hold that money has an absolute right to go wherever the highest return on investment can be secured.

The pastoral has much more of the same, to the point that, as one commentator has suggested, if put into practice 'we would have a social as well as a cultural revolution'. I recall one pithy observation on our behaviour to the travelling minority:

> 'We expect them to be good neighbours, yet many refuse to recognise them as neighbours …'

In the long run, of course:

> 'Justice does not happen … it has to be willed and worked for … *Neither will a just society necessarily or automatically come from general economic growth.*' (My italics)

Shades of the Celtic Tiger! In the meantime, thank God for those diehards who, from the socialist remnant to CORI, preach the need for a political will for justice.

A final word on culture and tradition – not least in relation to language and literature. (I have hardly referred to music or the visual arts. Not that I don't recognise their importance!)

I believe the Gaelic element in our cultural identity will survive and flourish. Institutionally it's going through a bad time at the moment (as is the church – but *it* has a Guarantor). I pin my faith on two positive developments. One has to do with our participation in the European Union: as political action becomes more centralised, the significance of cultural diversity must become more deeply valued. Second, and maybe more important, is a growing *ecological* consciousness over the past thirty years or so. We rightly mourn and condemn the neglect or destruction of any example of the diversity of creation: surely we will come to see the unique value of every one of the world's languages, those irreplaceable stores of value – and particularly our own.

One of the discoveries or rediscoveries of Vatican II which became a buzz-word of the post-conciliar church is, or was, *inculturation*. I hope it hasn't already been forgotten; it deserves remembering. And it doesn't apply only to Africa or Asia: it means more than 'native' liturgical dancing.

As far as Ireland is concerned, it would mean another rediscovery, another return to our roots. Not living in the past, but *with* the past, in the present, for the future.

Notes:
1. T. Ó Fiaich, 'The Beginnings of Christianity (5th and 6th Centuries)', in T. W. Moody and F. X. Martin (eds), *The Course of Irish History*, Mercier Press, Cork and Dublin, 1966, p 68.
2. 'Irish Monks on the Continent', in J. P. Mackey (ed), *An Introduction to Celtic Christianity*, T & T Clark, Edinburgh, 1989, p 132.
3. 'Wrestling with Ó Bruadair' in S. MacRéamoinn (ed), *The Pleasures of Gaelic Poetry*, Allen Lane, London, 1982, pp 63ff.

Lost Voices

Donal Flanagan

The New Testament takes a more optimistic view of the presence of the Spirit in the church than the voices of authority and institution. 'To each is given the manifestation of the Spirit for the common good' is what St Paul writes in 1 Cor 12:7, while in 1 Peter 4, we read: 'Like good stewards of the manifold grace of God, serve one another with whatever gift each of you has received.' Peter then adds the caution: 'Whoever speaks must do so as one speaking the very words of God, whoever serves must do so with the strength that God supplies, so that God may be glorified in all things through Jesus Christ' (vv 10-11).

The prophetic is a profound strand in Christian religious history. The loss of the prophetic voice is a constant hazard, not always avoided in the Christian centuries.

Religious history makes clear that religious institution needs the prophetic and that without it, institution itself becomes overblown, arrogant, even triumphalist in its self-presentation to the world. For its full health, institutional Christianity needs the prophetic. Once a religious institution, be it church, chapel or congregation, acquires a sense of institutional self-sufficiency it is already losing its way. The only way back is reform and a new attempt to listen for the prophetic voice. A religious institution such as the church can suffer this sclerosis at any point in its history or in any aspect of its work. The history of the church is replete with examples.

The prophetic voice
'No prophet is ever accepted in his own country' was what Jesus said of himself to his fellow citizens of Nazareth. It is a statement

that has been applied often to other and lesser men. The rejection of the prophet by his own seems to be a universal human
experience.

In many places in the New Testament 'ears to hear' are demanded. The Parable of the Sower calls forth such a challenge
(Mk 4:9), as does the lamp under the bushel (Mk 4:23). It is an
oft-repeated theme. Its frequency would suggest that Jesus
found a notable reluctance in his listeners to hear what he was
actually saying, and that this difficulty was not confined to the
ordinary folk among his audiences but touched his close disciples also. Why else would he say in Mark 8:18f to those closest to
him: 'Do you not yet perceive or understand? Are your hearts
hardened? Having eyes do you not see and having ears do you
not hear?'

This, indeed, was no new phenomenon in Israel as the words
of the prophet Ezechiel, which are echoed in the words of Jesus,
make clear. In Ezechiel 12:1f we read: 'The word of the Lord
came to me: Son of man you dwell in the midst of a rebellious
house who have eyes to see but see not, who have ears to hear
but hear not.' These words must have echoed in the mind of the
rejected prophet of Nazareth when his countrymen turned their
backs on him and closed their ears to his message.

The experience of Jesus' disciples was not too different from
his own as they moved out to preach his gospel in the aftermath
of Pentecost. Certainly the repetition, in the last book of the New
Testament, of the phrase, 'He who has an ear, let him hear what
the Spirit says to the churches', suggests that the same problem
confronted the early Christian preachers.

Chapter 2 of the Book of Revelation repeats four times the
phrase, 'He who has an ear, let him hear what the Spirit says to
the churches.' This chapter, which addresses the churches of
Ephesus, Smyrna, Pergamum and Thyatira, closes on the same
phrase, which is repeated to each of the churches individually in
the section of the chapter devoted to that church (See Rev 2:7, 11,
17, 29).

In Chapter 3, the same phrase is addressed to the churches of

Sardis, Philadelphia and Laodicea and, significantly, it is the closing phrase in the address to each church.

The Church Catholic carries the same obligation to listen to what the Spirit says to the church as did the seven churches of Asia Minor long ago. The Second Vatican Council, following Paul's words in 1 Corinthians, makes reference to the special graces which the Spirit distributes among the faithful (*Lumen Gentium* 12). Pointing out that Paul says: 'The manifestation of the Spirit is given to everyone for profit' (1 Cor 12:7), the Council continues: 'These charismatic gifts, whether they be the most outstanding or the more simple and widely diffused, are to be received with thanksgiving and consolation for they are exceedingly suitable and useful for the needs of the church' (*Lumen Gentium* 12).

Among the gifts of the Spirit given to the members of the people of God is prophecy. This is a continuation of Christ's prophetic office in the people of God, the power to bear witness to the gospel. Bearing witness to the gospel can sometimes occasion difficulties for those in authority in the church. And they, in their turn, may find it difficult to listen to prophetic witness. If they listen, listening without hearing is still a possibility, even for those who are in office in the church.

A prophetic Irish voice?

At the end of his 'Biographical Memoir' prefixed to the abridged version of Walter McDonald's *Reminiscences of a Maynooth Professor*, Denis Gwynn writes:

> It is too early yet to estimate how far Dr McDonald's views and efforts have found support in the decisions of the Vatican Council. But his demand that any priest should be informed of the grounds for suppressing his books and given the opportunity to defend himself has been definitely approved. His objection to the use of Latin in teaching and examinations in seminaries has gained wide support and approval. And his general ideas about the need for wider scope in clerical education have shown him to be a prophet in his day.[1]

During his student days in Maynooth, McDonald was a critic of the courses provided in the college. His nearly forty-year career as a teacher at Maynooth saw this same critical charism showing itself in ever broader fields. The last chapter of the *Reminiscences* was written after he received the medical report that told him he had only a short time to live. The final paragraphs of this chapter, his testament and valediction to those he had long confronted, is tinged with sorrow yet alive with hope. The final paragraph runs:

I have done my best and the result will be found in great part in the unpublished books which I leave behind … For some such thoughts the time is not ripe but it will come.

McDonald continues:

I should dearly love to see these volumes published but must pass away without hope of that. They might do a little to withstand the revolution which the official guardians of our religion will not see coming or will endeavour to keep out with their broomsticks. Good men, animated by the best of motives but so short-sighted and so cruel, too, in their religious blindness to such as cannot shut their eyes. So God permits – no doubt for wise purposes; blessed always be His holy will.' (op. cit., pp 268-269)

And again:

Episcophobia! Yes, I have faced Bishops and their Masters being worsted in the conflict and, as I believe, injured grievously. Not maliciously, however; the men who struck hardest at me did it in good faith. I do not blame them nor desire to see them punished, however I may feel aggrieved.

May they live long and rule happily, but may they be punished also, by having their eyes opened to the evil they had done unwittingly, not to me only – for that counts little – but to the cause of Truth. The shame of such revelation when it comes, as come it will, is more than enough of punishment.' (op. cit., p 269)

Facing death at peace and with confidence he writes:

I am to die soon; and, perhaps, as Lochiel's bard thought, in the sunset of life we may be gifted with special insight into the future, somewhat akin to prophetic vision; or, at least, a dying man may utter warnings with more effect than if he had promise of many years before him.' (op. cit., p 265)

Walter McDonald was a doughty fighter, a man ahead of his time. He was a prophet who read the 'signs of the times' fifty years before that expression became common currency in the debates surrounding Vatican II. McDonald died on May 2, 1920 and is buried in an unadorned grave in the college cemetery in Maynooth. The simple stone on his grave draws our attention to the fact that he died on the feast of St Athanasius. The phrase *Athanasius contra mundum* is loosely rendered as 'one, resolute man facing universal opposition'. Surely a fitting description of McDonald! And then Athanasius, who stood alone against the Arian heresy, was vindicated by its downfall. A lot that has happened since McDonald's death has borne out the prophetic character of much that he said. His words, not heeded by the monolithic official church of his time, have broken through to our day, as ecclesiastical certainties wilt and a faith with questions comes more and more into its own.

In his lifetime McDonald found himself cast in the part of the honest outsider, a lonely role in the church which followed Vatican I. Born in 1855, he was of the same generation as the virulent and extremist Msgr Umberto Benigni, the spider who sat at the centre of the web called the *Sodalitium Pianum*, the worldwide underground spying agency he founded and ran from Rome to uphold the secretive clericalist version of the church and of the gospel which he believed in. Here was a man for whom modernity was modernism.

McDonald, commenting on Maynooth theologians' attempts to start the *Irish Theological Quarterly* in 1907, writes: 'We were unfortunate in the time at which our project was commenced, as the Modernists not only lamed but killed us. They aimed at progress, so did we, therefore we were modernists ... Is it not a strange, sad thing that I, who not only hate modernism but feel a contempt for it, should be classed as a Modernist by so many, even high-placed ecclesiastics, as I know I am. The Modernists have set back the hands of progress in the church dear knows how many years – far beyond my time, I expect …'

And in a typical McDonald shot: 'It was hypocritical and mean of Loisy and Tyrrell to pretend to remain in the church.'

McDonald's courage, outspokenness and instinct for fair play stand in stark contrast to the secretive, underhand, code-laden meanness – to use a McDonald word – of Monsignor Benigni and his minions in the passageways of the Vatican.

The methods of the Roman crusade against modernism were inept and unCatholic. They represented a futile clericalist attempt which ignored the real challenge of the modern world and failed to define precisely the theological errors of modernism. It was so much simpler by the use of clerical scattershot to lame – another McDonald word – those who were trying to come to terms with the twentieth century. That honest efforts at *aggiornamento* (to use a term of one of the modernist suspects, later Pope John XXIII) were set back years, is an indisputable fact. That many fine scholars had their reputations blackened by lesser men sending in their twisted messages to the centre of the spider's web is a fact. That Catholic scholarship was placed in a state of suspended animation for a generation or more is a fact we cannot now alter, but should by no means forget or allow to fall from our memories.

McDonald's courage stands out against the background of the Roman crusade against modernism with its futile reliance on an encoded secrecy and the encouragement of delation, i.e. telling on one's friends, colleagues and neighbours or indeed anyone.

This campaign had as its aim the unattainable goal of carrying traditional ways, practices and opinions through to an unchanging and unchangeable future in the opening years of the twentieth century. The unfinished issues of the Pope of the *Syllabus* and of infallibility, the downturn of the last years of Leo XIII, came to full flowering in the intransigence of Pius X and his helper, Msgr Benigni, the scourge of modernity!

Yet, for all his adventuresome spirit, McDonald was obedient. Here was a man who could write in the final and valedictory chapter of his memoirs:

Few professors I dare to say – in all humility – have left in our college a record fairer than mine, of obedience to the rules and regulations made by the Trustees, wherever these rules did not in my opinion conflict with some more important and urgent principle. No President found me insubordinate or disrespectful, though I have resisted Presidents as has been shown. So, too, I have stood up to Bishops and even to the Holy See but reverently, I hope, and in the exercise of right. We are subjects but not slaves of episcopal and papal authority. (*Reminiscences*, 1966 ed., pp 262-3)

On a large map of church and world, McDonald may appear today as only a minor prophet. But he showed the marks of the calling, felt the pain and endured the failure without flinching. It is this which makes him a paradigmatic figure among Irish Catholic voices which have been unlistened to, unheeded, lost.

A voice before her time – Nano Nagle

Nano Nagle's work with the schooling of the Catholic poor of Cork, and their instruction in their religion, began sometime around 1750, possibly in 1754. Her little schools grew in number so that by 1769 she was engaged in seven schools in the city. In addition to working in these schools and supervising them, she provided from family resources for the upkeep of the schools and for the payment of those who taught in them. Money was also needed for her work with the sick poor in their own homes. When her own resources did not meet the demands of her varied works, she begged – and rich friends supplemented her income.

When Nano Nagle opened her first school in Cork, two things were uppermost in her mind: the poor of Cork and their great need for instruction in the Catholic faith. In addition to work in her schools, Nano found time to visit the sick, the aged and the poor in their homes. Her educational work was not focused only on the classroom. She was well aware of the desperate domestic circumstances from which many of her pupils came. It was necessary to get to know the parents of her scholars and to help them if she was to give her young pupils a real chance of improvement in life.

The first effort to place her work on a permanent basis was bringing the Ursulines to Cork, but their strict rule of enclosure severely limited their ability to help the 'poor schools'. It may be that Nano had hoped her foundation would adopt a more out-going policy, like some Ursuline foundations on the continent, but this was not to be. Thus, early in 1775 at the age of 57, in order to give the permanence required to work for her 'poor scholars', she started a new grouping – the Sisters of the Charitable Instruction of the Sacred Heart of Jesus. Nano Nagle was the first superior of the grouping.

It was Nano's intent that the sisters of her society would continue her work among the poor of the city, with a special focus on poverty. They would not be enclosed religious like the Ursulines. Her friend and collaborator, Dr Moylan, Bishop of Cork, fought long and hard battles with the Roman authorities to get recognition for the new congregation to work on the lines taken by Nano a quarter of a century earlier. This time, it would not be a personal and individual apostolate with paid helpers, but a concerted effort by a religious community animated by Nano's ideals and spirit. The name she chose for her little new company is a revealing one. It points back to the twenty-five years of Nano's work in instruction and compassion for the poor. It points forward to the future of the new community which was taking up her work. In this venture, Nano obviously wished the sisters to live and work with the same freedom she had enjoyed and the same dedication she had brought to the work. In this she had the strong support of Bishop Moylan. The bright optimism of the new venture may be seen in one of the submissions he made to Rome – this on the question of enclosure:

It is objected that enclosure is not to be observed. Though this may seem to be a matter full of apprehension yet if their Eminences had an intimate knowledge of the conditions of this country they would not see so much difficulty.

In the first place, it must be remembered that perfect enclosure does not exist in this country; the religious women of various orders are accustomed to go out for reasons approved by the superior. Again, it must be observed that our women, not only religious but those recognised as pious, are much attached to chastity and averse to worldly cares. Enclosure and iron grilles are not more staunch than their sterling dispositions. Nevertheless, since human nature is frail and liable to fall, and because in such an important matter care must be taken against every appearance and danger of evil, the Sisters will be prohibited from going out except in accordance with the attached statutes. The safeguard appears to me to be quite sufficient.

Dr Moylan's pointed insistence on the needs and the challenge of Irish conditions was apparently lost on the Cardinals and advisers of Propaganda Fide. His support for Nano's new project counted for nothing against Roman intransigence. Her prophetic inspiration to give the nuns the freedom of movement which their mission demanded was lost in a welter of canonical caution and patriarchal concern. One more new voice unheard in the name of Christian propriety. Or was it just convention?

Diaspora

Nano Nagle represented a prophetic new beginning in the style of Catholic evangelisation in late eighteenth-century Ireland. In the event it transpired that neither Rome nor the newly prosperous yet fearful Catholic middle classes of Cork were ready for this startling but necessary innovation.

This is perhaps not be be wondered at in a people which had lived a dubious legal existence in their own country since at least the beginning of the eighteenth century, and many of whose brightest scholars had found homes in the universities, schools and religious houses of Europe for a considerable time before that. This outflow had left the Catholic community in Ireland bereft of many fine talents. In spite of their success in Spain, France, the Low Countries and the Austrian Empire, they must count as voices lost to the church in their homeland. Their going cannot but have altered the character of that church.

It is customary to praise the real achievements of Irish clergy on the Continent between 1600 and the 1789 French Revolution. These achievements are substantial and cannot be gainsaid. It is necessary, however, to keep in mind that the price of this success was a church in Ireland deprived of such voices. Exile removed them from experiencing at first hand their Catholic faith in their own land. They could write learned tomes in the libraries of Europe and gain scholarly fame, but they could not endure in their own bodies the pain of banishment and internal exile we find in *An Díbirt go Connachta* (Exile to Connacht). Nor could they write it down for us to read.

It is not possible for us today to say what these scholars would have done had they remained in Ireland. Nor can we recreate their voices as if they had never left these shores. We can, however, by looking at their talents and achievements, see that, by their going, the Irish scene was deprived of a valued voice whose contribution we shall now never know. We can still mourn their lost voices.

The names of this great diaspora of the seventeenth and eighteenth centuries are very many. Their careers are varied, their locations in Europe also. A small selection may give some idea of the Irish Catholic community's loss through the persecuting history that shaped those men's lives and sent them into exile.

When many years ago I first came across the name of Johannes Sinnichius in a moral theology text book, I was unaware that this Latin veil concealed an Irishman from Cork called Shinnick. Born in Cork in 1603, he died in Louvain in 1666. Professor for Philosophy and Theology at the university in 1635, he was its Rector Magnificus in 1642. A close associate of Cornelius Jansen (+1638) he assisted in the posthumous publication of Jansen's *Augustinus*, a work destined to stir up most serious doctrinal controversies. Shinnick was sent to Rome 1643-45, to defend the university position which was favourable to Jansen. He also wrote a series of dogmatic works under pseudonyms defending the Jansenist position. When the definitive condemnation of Innocent X in the Bull *Cum occasione* received the Royal *placet* in the Low Countries, Shinnick seems to have accepted this. We find no further dogmatic writings from his pen after this date. In his later writings he pursued a rigorist line in moral theology.

Another Corkman, born in the same year as John Shinnick, was John Punch who became a Franciscan. He entered the Order at St Anthony's College, Louvain. He studied philosophy at Cologne and theology at Louvain and Rome. He taught in Rome, Lyons and Paris. He was a significant figure in the revival of Scotist studies in the seventeenth century and was recognised as a faithful and acute exponent of the philosophy and theology of John Duns Scotus. He died 1672.

Bonaventure Baron was another scholar of the Diaspora. Born in Clonmel in 1610, his mother was Mary Wadding, a sister of Fr Luke Wadding. Bartholomew Baron, professed as a Franciscan with the name Bonaventure, did his novitiate at Timoleague Abbey in Cork. Later, he studied in Louvain, Augsburg and Salzburg, before taking his theology at St Isidore's in Rome. He worked in various Franciscan houses in Europe as the publication of his writings in Cologne, in Wurzburg and in Rome indicate. Aged 86, he died in Rome in 1696. A Franciscan writer refers to him as 'one of the leading humanists of the age, a great scholastic philosopher and theologian, and an elegant writer of history and biography.'[2]

From Sicily to Poland, from Cadiz to Prague, we find Irish clergy, secular and regular, teaching all over Europe in the seventeenth century. They are recorded for example at ten centres in Italy, six in France, five in Spain and six in the Hapsburg Empire. They are found not just in major centres like Rome, Paris, Louvain, Cologne and Salamanca, but also in Brindisi, Prague, Segovia, Valladolid, Palermo, Syracuse, Klosterneuburg near Vienna, Graz, Bözen (Tyrol) and in many other places. Their presence is Europe's gain. It is also Ireland's loss. These are casualties of our stormy religious history. Voices speaking in exile, lost voices.

In the seventeenth century struggle of Irish Catholicism to survive, there were many lost voices. Not just those seeking refuge in exile but also those who dared to return from Europe in this violent century. They too must count as lost voices. They often paid the ultimate price.

Richard Synott was born in Wexford around 1590. He first went to the Irish College, Lisbon, along with Luke Wadding. In 1604 both entered a Franciscan Novitiate near Oporto. Both studied philosophy at Leira and theology at Lisbon and Coimbra. Synott returned to Ireland in 1613 joining the Irish Province. In 1633 Wadding invited him to become Guardian of the newly-begun foundation of St Isidore's in Rome, but he only remained there one year, resigning for health reasons and returning to Ireland.

In 1649 Cromwell laid siege to Wexford. A military dispatch, drawn up five days after the capture of the city, reads as follows:

We lay before this city eight days and on the ninth day which was the eleventh of this month God delivered it and the strong castle thereof into our hands ... God visited both the deceivers and the deceived together. Of their priests which deceived and led them were many slain. Some (I heard of) came holding forth crucifixes before them and conjuring our soldiers (for His sake who saved us all), to save their lives; yet our soldiers would not own their dead images for our living Saviour but struck them dead with their idols. Many of their priests being got together in a Church of the town (where, 'tis said, many poor Protestants were kept and killed together in the beginning of the Rebellion) were slain together by our soldiers about their altars.'[3]

Richard Synott, with six other Franciscans, died in the massacre at Wexford.

So many lost voices.

Notes:

1. Walter McDonald, *Reminiscences of a Maynooth Professor*, Edited with a Memoir by Denis Gwynn, Cork: Mercier Press. 1967, p 54.

2. Quoted in Gregory Cleary, OFM, *Father Luke Wadding and St Isidore's College, Rome. Biographical and Historical Notes and Documents*, Rome 1925, p 92.

3. Cleary, op. cit., pp 152-3.

Liberal Democracy, Crisis and the Christian Vision

Gabriel Daly OSA

The twentieth century has seen two powerful movements which believed that history has a goal: Nazism and Communism. Their followers pursued their goals with passionate conviction and, when they had power, with ruthless and totalising determination. These movements were like secular religions, demanding not less than everything from their adherents. Both failed; and their passing has left an ideological vacuum. This is the central thesis of a book which was published nearly a decade ago under the title *The End of History and the Last Man*.[1] The author is Francis Fukuyama, a former deputy director of the US State Department's Policy Planning Staff.

It is a profoundly secular book which asks about the direction of history, of human culture, and of political ambitions. It reflects on the fall of two totalitarianisms in the twentieth century. It settles finally, and *faute de mieux,* for the attainment of liberal democracy as the final goal of all human striving. Liberal democracy, for all its failings, says Fukuyama, 'in reality constitutes the best possible solution to the human problem.'[2] When it is finally attained worldwide, history will have ended. There will be no great causes left to fight for.

The bathos of this thesis could lead one to dismiss it as vacuous and boring; but it is probably as representative a contemporary diagnosis of Western culture as one might find anywhere. There are many worse conditions than liberal democracy, and in fairness to Fukuyama it should be noted that he does not relish the prospect he puts forward for our consideration:

The end of history will be a very sad time. The struggle for recognition, the willingness to risk one's life for a purely abstract goal, the worldwide ideological struggle that called forth daring, courage, imagination, and idealism, will be replaced by economic calculation, the endless solving of technical problems, environmental concerns, and the satisfaction of sophisticated consumer demands. In the post-historical period there will be neither art nor philosophy, just the perpetual caretaking of the museum of human history.

Fukuyama is of course using 'history' in a specialised – some might say eccentric – sense, but it is a sense which should engage the attention of Christians. For him history without ideological commitment is hollow. This is an implicit challenge to Christianity, which from its inception has always claimed to make transcendent sense of the world.

Fukuyama has just written another book entitled *The Great Disruption: Human Nature and the Reconstruction of Social Order*,[3] in which he argues that the move from the industrial age to information-based technology has been accompanied by a large-scale decline in moral standards (the 'great disruption'). Writing out of what appears to be cultural panic, he issues a call for the reconstruction of moral standards. Liberal democracy is under threat from crime, from the breakdown of the family and from other social ills. All allies in the struggle against social disintegration are welcome, including religion. He is not in the least concerned with the truth or falsehood of religious claims. God plays no part in his thinking.

He describes with approval what he calls 'instrumental religion': 'That is, the practice of religion is sustained not by dogmatic belief in revelation but rather because religious teachings constitute a convenient language in which to express the community's existing moral rules.'[4] This unashamed utilitarianism, which treats religion as no more than a prop and language-provider to social ethics, fits in with the death of history as described in Fukuyama's earlier book. It is fashionably postmodern to the extent that Fukuyama's world eschews the transcendent vision of most religions, including Christianity. Liberal democracy's highest ideal is the right to be left alone.[5]

Most of Fukuyama's examples come from the USA, which, as he points out, disproves the common European sociological contention that modernity and secularisation necessarily kill off religious practice. His superficial treatment of religion does not allow him to analyse the reasons for the persistence of religious practice in the USA. He is evidently happy as long as religion underwrites the social morality which is needed for liberal democracy to function.

I have chosen Fukuyama's bland and passionless scenario as a convenient foil to the vision which sustained and stimulated the first Christians, many of whom did indeed believe that history was coming to an end. They, however, meant something very different from Fukuyama's 'end of history'. They believed that the Lord was coming to judge the world and to give history its final meaning. Their timescale was wrong, but time itself soon cured that.

The Jesus movement, which burgeoned into a congeries of regional 'churches', began its existence in the turbulence of several large and radical crises which make our contemporary crises look tame. First and foremost was the cruel death of Jesus of Nazareth on a cross outside Jerusalem, which left his friends and disciples leaderless and still awaiting the end of history. Then came the crisis of their encounter with Jesus alive again though clearly living on a different plane of existence. What were they to make of a crucified and risen Messiah? Deep theological questions clamoured for an answer.

Contingent tragedy or divine plan?

There was the basic and critical dilemma which faced the disciples of Jesus (and which continues to challenge Christians today): was the brutal fact of what happened on Golgotha a simple contingent event of history, or was it divinely willed? Each alternative had its possibilities and its drawbacks. Today we may not feel as constrained to choose between these two alternatives as the first Christians did. Many contemporary theologians would prefer to tackle the problem of how to combine the historical contingency of Golgotha with the divine will rather than treating them as mutually exclusive. The early church, as depicted by Luke in *Acts of the Apostles*, saw the matter as a choice between two exclusive alternatives. Peter's Pentecost speech to the crowd, as recorded by Luke in the 2nd chapter of Acts, rejected the very idea that the crucifixion of Jesus was an accidental event ...

> [Jesus], handed over to you according to the definite plan and foreknowledge of God, you crucified and killed by the hands of those outside the law. But God raised him up, having freed him from death, because it was impossible for him to be held in its power. (Acts 2:23-4)

This firm rejection of random historicity free of divine control committed the Christian Church and its theologians to a continuing search for transcendent meaning in the death of Jesus. The creeds would shortly proclaim that Jesus died 'for us and for our salvation' – a phrase which answered one theological question while raising several others. (Theories of atonement soon became common both among theologians and in popular piety.)

The arrival on the Christian scene of Paul of Tarsus dramatised and deepened an already critical situation. Paul was a one-man crisis in himself. His theology was done on the hoof, and it remains a constant reminder that the best theology often comes from reflection on the problems thrown at the theologian by history, by the lived-world and by culture in general. Paul had practical problems to meet as he brought the good news of Christ to the Gentile world. First there was the delayed return of the Lord. Paul's flock at Thessalonica were asking awkward questions about this. It is not easy for Christians today to share imaginatively in the cast of mind of their first-century forbears who were expecting the return of Jesus at any moment. The non-fulfilment of their expectation constituted a crisis which gradually cleared with the passage of time.

The second crisis which faced Paul, and through him the rest of the early church, was the practical pastoral question of

whether Gentile converts to Christianity should be subjected to
the Jewish Law. Paul said no, thereby putting conviction before
institutional convenience and threatening the unity of the Jesus
movement. He stood up to Peter and employed arguments of
immense theological power and penetration to justify his missionary programme. According to Luke in Acts 17, Paul tried
some academic apologetics in Athens where easily-bored intellectuals gave him a perfunctory hearing and told him to come
back again some time. The fact that this languid and dilettantish
atmosphere did not prove receptive to Paul's gospel illustrates
Max Weber's tart observation, 'No matter how much the appearance of a widespread religious interest may be simulated,
no new religion has ever resulted from the needs of intellectuals
nor from their chatter.'[6]

Corinth, to which Paul went next, was a very different sort of
place. It has been nicely described by Jerome Murphy-O'Connor
as 'a wide-open boomtown' not unlike San Francisco during the
Californian gold rush.[7] Unlike Athens, Corinth was all too passionate. Crises were guaranteed here. Yet Corinth proved unexpectedly to be fertile soil for the good news of salvation. The
Corinthians found Paul's teaching vibrant, exciting and contro-
versial. Paul learned much about them and about himself from
his dealings with them. In Corinth there were factions, jeal-
ousies, sexual licence and highly enthusiastic forms of worship –
in short, considerable scope for redemption. Paul observed and
gave judgement in difficult cases such as eating meat sacrificed
to idols and speaking in tongues. Amid all this turmoil he produced some of his finest theology. 1 Cor 13, which is at once
poetry, moral exhortation, hard-headed theological reflection
and practical instruction to his flock, is as incandescent today as
it must have seemed to the Corinthian Christians who heard it
read at their assemblies.

Amid all his difficulties, Paul was conscious of having a marvellous message to preach which is 'the light that is knowledge
of the glory of God in the face of Jesus Christ' (2 Cor 4:6). We
preach Christ crucified, an offence to Jews and folly to Gentiles

(1 Cor 1:23). What we preach is a treasure. 'But we have only clay jars to hold this treasure, and this proves that such transcendent power does not come from us; it is God's alone' (2 Cor 4:7). Time and again in the succeeding centuries the fragile jars would be shattered by neglect of the truth that the power is God's alone and that it needs no human defences. Indeed it seems to flourish in times of crisis.

The cost of 'Establishment'

For the first three centuries of Christian history there was little danger that this lesson of the sovereignty of God's grace would be forgotten. Christians were a sporadically persecuted minority, and for the most part social and political outsiders. Then, with the conversion of Constantine in the early fourth century, a far-reaching and radical change took place. Persecution ceased and Christians were welcomed into full membership of the Empire. By the end of the fourth century, Christianity had become the established imperial church with the power and privilege which normally attend such establishment. There were Christians who viewed what had happened with alarm and disapproval. Those who profess to follow the poor and powerless Jesus, they felt, should not invoke or associate with the sort of power which had brought about the suffering and death of the Founder of Christianity.

In the centuries which succeeded the Constantinian revolution, Christianity became Christendom, in which the culture of Europe was shaped by the narratives and symbols of Christian belief. The resultant art, architecture, music and literature are among the glories of the human imagination and are a lasting witness to the tradition which inspired them.

On the darker side, however, were the abuses of power, and the readiness of Christian leaders to resort to worldly politics and even violence to promote their doctrinal and moral teaching, to say nothing of their nakedly political ends. Popes became monarchs and bishops became princes. War was waged on Muslims and Jews, especially during the crusades. The Inquisition became an instrument of enforced uniformity. The

Eastern and Western Churches broke the bonds of unity and love between them. Western Christianity was fragmented in the sixteenth century, and the grim effects can still be seen in Northern Ireland. The list could be prolonged, but these instances are enough to illustrate the Pauline observation that our treasure is in fragile vessels, and to suggest that the crises that face us in the third millennium offer opportunities to retrieve something of the vision with which the crises of the early church were met.

The Christian Church has shown from the start that it can thrive on crises as long as these crises are genuinely religious or moral. If they are predominantly institutional, however, the situation is much less healthy. The Roman Catholic Church in the nineteenth and early twentieth centuries saw itself as under siege by the modern world. It gathered its wagons into a tight circle and proclaimed modernity in all its forms to be the enemy. The papacy set out to centralise authority in its own hands and to crush any attempt by Catholic scholars to enter into dialogue with modern culture. As a result, Rome became ever more preoccupied with its own authority as an object of religious faith; the medium became the message; and the reputation of the church as institution came to matter more than the rights and needs of people. The church was virtually identified with the kingdom preached by Jesus, instead of being seen as the servant of the kingdom.

From the middle of the nineteenth century, the Roman Catholic Church in Ireland found itself heir to both Constantinian power and influence and to the centralising tactics of an anti-modern papacy. With the birth of the new state in 1922, the church achieved effortless influence in Irish social and political life. Apart from some literary anti-clericalism, the church had never, until the 1990s, encountered serious opposition or hostility of the type which was commonplace on the Continent since the eighteenth century. It was not well fitted to meet the challenge of the New Ireland, and it was tragically unprepared to respond to the scandals which have rocked it in the last decade of the twentieth century.

It has not simply fallen out of its standing; it has fallen from a pedestal where it had little reason to be self-critical. The long tradition of putting the institution before the claims of truth and justice is at the core of the recent scandals. An ingrained sense of the need to protect the good name of the church prevented many churchpeople from recognising the superior need for re-form of attitudes. When the scandals made the demand for that reform unavoidable, its agent was not the church itself but the communications media.

The sad fact has been that the media have done what the church seemed unable or unwilling to do for itself. That the media have been at times viciously hostile, self-indulgent and unjust should not be allowed to detract from the importance of the task they have performed. The church owes them a debt of pained gratitude for what they have done.

Responsible and critically-minded churchpeople recognise that modern journalism has an important role to play in the preservation of public honesty and freedom, by its readiness to run a story or article which is of public interest but which will embarrass those, including churchpeople, who hold power in society. Where a church has held unchallenged power, it can ex-pect today to be the legitimate object of journalistic attention. In the past in Ireland the media did not perform their role of critical reporting and commenting on church matters. They were defer-ential and all too ready to collude in the establishment power game. One reason why some church authorities in Ireland are so instinctively hostile to the media is the bewildering rapidity and radical character of the change which has taken place. It seems only yesterday that they had effortless impunity and freedom from public criticism. It is as if your tame poodle had become a ferocious life-threatening animal overnight. Suddenly the land is full of aspiring Woodwards and Bernsteins in feverish search of ecclesiastical Watergates.

Through the instrumentality of the media, the Catholic Church in Ireland has been humiliated and discredited. It can react in either of two ways. It can follow the wretched precedent of circling the wagons and resentfully nursing its wounds, or it can recognise that here is a God-given opportunity to experience and speak of the deepest Christian truths with greater authenticity and effectiveness than it was able to do when it was unchallenged and confident. It will no longer be able to lay down the law with impunity, as it did in the past and as its Roman masters would like it to continue to do; but it will be able to commend, to listen, to discuss and, when appropriate, to debate on the basis of equality, together with members of other churches and also with the increasing number of unchurched.

In an authoritarian church, with inadequate means for open and fearless internal communication, these qualities are not easy to acquire, but in a broken church it could be otherwise. In a time of humiliation it may prove easier to turn to the great redemptive truths of the Christian creed: God, creation, Christ, the Holy Spirit, grace, forgiveness and healing. These also happen to be the truths that Christians are called upon to profess in a world increasingly self-limited to the vision of liberal democracy as an ultimate goal.

Domesticating religion

Fukuyama's ideal world does not at first sight look very threatening or inimical to Christianity. Its very blandness, however, conceals its contradiction of much that Christianity stands for. How one lives as a Christian and witnesses to Christ in such a world remains a challenging question, not unlike the questions that faced Christians after the Constantinian revolution. Liberal democracy, shored up by conservative economics in a period of prosperity, is unlikely to be solicitous for the needs of the poor and marginalised in society, unless those needs are continually brought to public attention. Liberation theology has the distinction of creating the phrase, 'preferential option for the poor'. In a booming economy few options are likely to favour the poor, and it will fall in part to church bodies to keep pointing this out, thereby irritating right-wing economists and politicians in government at the time. (To irritate right-wing economists may well be a function of practising the Christian gospel, though it is important that the prophetic Christian should be economically literate, lest the gospel message be damaged by professional incompetence.)

Fukuyama's sponsorship of 'instrumental religion' raises the question of the relationship between religion and morality and especially of the dependence of morality on religion for its plausibility and authenticity. If morality is heavily dependent on religion for its authentication, abandonment of religious faith can destroy moral plausibility structures. The Irish situation bears this out spectacularly. The last forty years have seen a cultural revolution from the profoundly conservative to an 'anything goes' attitude.

In a perceptive article in *The Irish Times*,[8] Dr Garret FitzGerald observed that there has been a fundamental shift in Irish culture from judgemental to non-judgemental attitudes. 'Only a generation ago we were unusually censorious – or we lived comfortably with censorious attitudes to departures from societal norms … Now there is an equally strong convention against expressing any view that could be considered to be "judgemental".' With the collapse of church authority there is an urgent need for civic morality to replace it, but, according to Dr FitzGerald, non-judgemental opinion-formers are hostile to such a development. This passage from one extreme to its opposite suggests a disconcerting dearth of intellectual seriousness in some at least of our opinion-formers.

Something similar is happening in the religious sphere. Organised religion, church dogma and regulated worship are seen to be suffering a calamitous reverse. However, there are signs that 'spirituality' is taking the place formerly occupied by church-based religion. No good purpose is served by reserving the word 'religion' for all the negative aspects of (organised) religion or by employing the word 'spirituality' for what is open, free and affirmative. It is better to recognise that there is good and bad, true and false religion, just as there is good and bad, true and false spirituality. It is salutory to remember that early Christians were persecuted for their 'atheism'. Words need a context for focused meaning.

The privatising of religion

Perhaps the subtlest threat of liberal democracy to Christian values is the privatising of religion. How else, the argument runs, can pluralism be protected from the totalising tendencies of organised religion than by declaring it to be just another private pursuit like hang-gliding, internet-surfing and ballroom dancing? Religion in this way of thinking must be left free, but it must be denied access to the processes of public decision-making. Suspicion of the influence of religion in public life is understandable in view of the grim history of religious intolerance and persecution of dissenters. It is surely a matter for shame that religious freedom in the Western world was inspired by secular liberalism rather then by the faith-inspired conviction that freedom is necessary for a fruitful reception of the gospel. Few measures were fought with greater determination and ferocity by the conservative minority during the Second Vatican Council than the Declaration on Religious Liberty. Churches need to remember their history when they seek a public hearing, as they have every right to do, in the contemporary world.

Nevertheless it is all too easy to pass from one extreme to its opposite. This has become evident in the USA where the First Amendment to the Constitution reads, 'Congress shall make no law respecting an establishment of religion, or prohibiting the free exercise thereof.' The eighteenth-century founding Fathers of the US were all too aware of the wars of religion in seventeenth-century Europe and were determined to ensure that nothing comparable should occur in their new nation. The First Amendment was formulated with that in mind. As Justice William Brennan pointed out, however, it is one thing to prescribe state neutrality towards religion; it is quite another to prevent state *neutrality* from become state *hostility* to religion in public life.

Various dedicated secularist and humanist societies campaign for the removal of religion from public life but fail to see that their own position is no less an ideology than religion is. The notion that secularism is neutral while religion is biased is patently absurd.

The privatising of religion contributes substantially to the fragmentation of society and the promotion of individualism. The churches can all too easily acquiesce in this process. It makes for a quieter and more hassle-free life. There are no hostile media to contend with, unless some scandal has got into the news. The pieties of church life can be pursued in peace by an ever dwindling church membership. Meanwhile secular life goes on uninfluenced by the kind of analysis, conversation and argument which a reflective religious faith can offer in freedom to the secular world. The consequences of this kind of withdrawal of religion and theology from public life ultimately amount to an abandonment of the Christian Church's commission to preach the gospel.

New challenges

Preaching the gospel at the turn of the new millennium, against the background of liberal democracy, means being as attentive to means as to ends. The challenge is how to present religious and moral ideals in a pluralistic setting while respecting the autonomy and authenticity of those who are being asked to listen. The Irish situation is particularly apposite here. The sheer rapidity of the revolution from conservative isolation to full membership of the Western capitalist world has left the Christian churches unsure of how to respond.

Dr Tony Fahey, research professor at the Economic and Social Research Institute, interprets the change as a progress from Catholicism and small-farm values, which were authoritarian and repressive, to a brave new world of 'egalitarian individualism'.[9] He appears to suggest that individualism is the only guarantor of 'the authentic self'. Again, he seems to imply that religion – or at any rate Catholicism – cannot fulfil this role. He concludes with a challenge to Christianity 'to recover the spiritual dimension of the self and re-inject it into daily cultural life.' Should Christianity accept this invitation?

Dr Fahey's 'egalitarian individualism' appears to have much in common with Fukuyama's 'liberal democracy', though what he understands by 'the spiritual dimension of the self' is not im-

mediately clear. Evidently Catholics and small farmers lack it. It
is emphatically secular. Is it the Cartesian self? If so, it is curiously
at odds with one of the leading orthodoxies of postmodern secular culture. Is it worth recovering? The egalitarian aspect of it is
certainly attractive, but the individualism is much less so.
Indeed it is the individualism of the New Ireland which one may
find repellent, especially when it expresses itself in greed, preoccupation with social (i.e. monetary) status, and disregard for
the needy.

The 'authentic self', so far from being individualistic, is relational.[10] It is formed, shaped and developed by personal and social contact with other people. This conviction is what Christians
need to proclaim, just as Paul did to his people in Corinth: 'Now
you are all Christ's body, and each of you a limb or organ of it' (1
Cor 12:27). Paul's imaginative vision is certainly egalitarian,
though it is in no way individualistic. His unruly flock at
Corinth undoubtedly contained many individualists – that was
in point of fact one of the problems they posed for him. His response was neither authoritarian nor individualistic. His aim was
to harness all the different temperaments, talents and energies to
serve the purposes of the one body. Each self would, he taught,
achieve its authenticity by contributing to the good of the whole
while preserving its own characteristic qualities. Paul's mystical
imagination suggested to him the model of Christ's body to de-
pict the society of Christian believers. Thus he was able to give
his people a relational model of morality which was rooted in a
mystical vision of their relationship with the risen Christ. It was
good crisis theology which remains as valid today as it was then.
If it can be recovered, there will be no need of some New Age
'spiritual dimension of the self'.

Tension between 'real' and 'ideal'
The real challenge which faces the Christian Church today is
how to hold out the ideal vision of God's kingdom as preached
by Jesus, while at the same time cherishing all those who for one
reason or another fall by the wayside or fail to meet the exacting

requirements of church membership, or who are tragic victims of their genetic, cultural and moral inheritance.

In the end, perhaps the greatest defect of Fukuyama's vision is its lack of a sense of the tragic element in life that comes about when human freedom encounters the restraints imposed by genetic inheritance, cultural deprivation, contingent misfortunes, and the constant friction between reason and feeling. Miguel de Unamuno, the distinguished Spanish philosopher of culture, called it 'the tragic sense of life'. It refuses to capitulate before the extremes of absolute predeterminism, on the one hand, or liberal optimism on the other. Instead it interprets human life as a field of contending energies without which we would not be truly human. Unamuno singles out some Christian thinkers who have been especially sensitive to the tragic sense of life, notably, Augustine, Pascal and Kierkegaard. These Christian thinkers, he claims, are burdened with wisdom rather than knowledge.[11] No one can be wise, he says, who gives no thought to the origin and destiny of human beings. 'And this supreme preoccupation cannot be purely rational, it must involve the heart. It is not enough to think about destiny: it must be felt.'[12]

Kierkegaard saw it as the paradox which is brought about in Christ by the conjunction of the human with the divine. Pascal saw it in the *fait intèrieur* which human beings encounter when they look with bewilderment into their own hearts and discover there what makes them the glory and the scandal of the universe. Augustine leads the way when, in his *Confessions*, he tries, under the influence of God's grace, to make sense of the contradictions built into his own inner life and discovers the disturbing experience of what it means to be human. One must be prepared to go deep enough into one's inner self and be not afraid to face the contradictions that all human beings encounter there: the unsatisfied aspirations, the moral ambivalence, the divided self, all of which go to make up the divine project which God the creator has completed in Jesus the Christ. Jesus called it the kingdom or reign of God and invited all, including especially the outcasts, to enter it. It makes nonsense of the claim that there are no great causes left, and it embodies an ideal vastly superior to 'egalitarian individualism'.

Notes:

1. London, 1992.
2. ibid., p 338.
3. London, 1999.
4. ibid., p 238.
5. William C. Placher, *Unapologetic Theology: A Christian Voice in a Pluralistic Conversation*, (Louisville, Kentucky, 1989), p 85.
6. M. Weber, *The Sociology of Religion*, (Boston, 1964), p 137.
7. J. Murphy-O'Connor, *Paul: A Critical Life*, (Oxford, 1996), p 108.
8. Saturday, Feb 13, 1999, p 14.
9. Tony Fahey, 'The Culture of Egalitarian Individualism in Modern Ireland', *Doctrine and Life* (May/June 1999), pp 258-66.
10. This point is well argued by Dr Dermot Lane who responds to Dr Fahey in the same issue of *Doctrine and Life*, ibid., pp 267-275.
11. Miguel de Unamuno, *Tragic Sense of Life*, (New York, 1954), p 18.
12. ibid., p 16.

The present crisis: a way forward?

Colm Kilcoyne

I'm sure all the churches in Ireland are having their difficulties and are doing some soul searching. My direct experience is of the Roman Catholic Church in the west of Ireland. This does not mean that the church I write about has no similarities with either Catholic life elsewhere in Ireland or with Christians of other denominations. What it does mean, though, is that I write about a church that has undergone massive upheaval in a few years. It is no time ago since we in this part of Ireland looked out, not just on foreign countries but at our own urbanised east, and wondered about social and religious earthquakes. Now the tremors have reached our own patch and pulled down much of what was familiar.

We, like others, have to search, if not for a return to a safe place, then certainly for new unmapped ways into the future.

The search

Jean Vanier says people are looking for a wisdom to guide their lives, rather than a church to belong to. We all search for a source to which we can entrust our hearts. Whatever releases meaning attracts allegiance.

The church claims to deliver meaning, to have privileged energies in its sacraments and teachings, to understand not only the human heart but also the mind of God as revealed in Jesus Christ. Of all the voices in the marketplace the church seems uniquely placed to claim credibility in the matter of releasing meaning into life.

For many, it is still making good its claim. Despite all, there is an awesome goodness within the church community. Away from the headlines, there are the anonymous people who live beautiful lives and get much of their power to do so from membership of the church. One of the unsung strengths of the church – and of our nation – is the subtle sanctity that Christianity continues to mediate for so many people.

But there is a strain developing, a growing tension between the sophistication of these people and the clumsiness of the institutional church.

When I talk about sophistication, I am *not* talking about crassness – where the new wealth and lifestyle have dulled awareness and made church involvement a social embarrassment.

What I *am* talking about are people who are both committed to the new Ireland and to their church. These are people who still have the happy feeling that the church has treasures that can enrich life. They have no desire to leave it; not one bit embarrassed by practising. They want it to work for them. They are comfortable with the church as their home. So far.

But it gets harder for them by the day. They often face tension in the home, disappointment with their families and the pressure of keeping up. Rahner calls this 'the experience of darkness'. He claims that this kind of personal experience, rather than technical arguments, often causes the deepest difficulties with Christianity. As a result, 'the spirit and the heart are dark, tired and despairing'.

Irish people were never anybody's fools but now, more than ever, they dare to ask the hard questions of all the institutions that touch their lives. They've grown used to accountability, to serious debate in the workplace and to the concept of competence in high places. They see no reason why the church should be exempt from any of these standards.

I suggest that this is where the vast majority of church members stand right now: wanting the church to be relevant; wishing their children to continue in the tradition; prepared to look beyond the scandals and the amateurism; willing the church out of its tiredness into some kind of vision that will give meaning to a jumbled and hectic new Ireland; aching for a simplicity that connects them with Jesus Christ.

Not all of us wake up every morning with these sombre thoughts about the church. We never were and never will be an island of fiercely intense saints. Few of us want religion as 'the be all and end all' of life.

Making Sense
But we want it to make sense, gospel sense. We realise that the values of the marketplace and those of Jesus Christ don't always match. We like it that way because we suspect the sanest place to walk is in the cracks between opposites.

What is happening now, I believe, is that life is getting so complex, so rushed, so full of new options, and our religion isn't keeping up. I don't mean trendy or blindly supportive of the culture. In fact, part of the self-imposed irrelevance of the church is that it doesn't come across as subversive enough – as challenging the culture in any kind of positive, gospel-based way. Rather, it comes across as just plain grumpy over people having fun and a few pounds in their pockets.

Many people still have an ease with the transcendent, a curiosity about mystery and an affection for what a clutter-free church could contribute to Irish life. Apart from the chronically critical who wish the church into oblivion, there is a nervousness that without an effective church we might collapse into some soulless future.

So, there is still a degree of faith and goodwill. What's the problem?

A matter of style, a case of content
I suggest it is about both style and content.

Take style. It has to do with how inviting is the church environment. How open to the culture without becoming its lap dog? How warm is its ritual without turning clap-happy? How well does it celebrate good fortune? Is it as deeply pro-life as it would like to present itself?

The perception – based on style – is that our church is mainly one that makes 'joy suspect and hope worthless'. *(Nietzche)*

Brian Moore starts one of his novels with the sentence: 'In the beginning was the Word and the Word was "No".' A hunch that religion is never happier than when it is chaining the spirit or clipping wings.

Liam O'Flaherty has a short story where he pictures a bronze eagle on a pulpit, staring down with stern eye. Above the eagle is the priest, also stern eyed. Both eagle and priest are dead to kindness, above the struggle. You could protest that this is cruel, warped stuff. Lazy stereotyping. You argue that the church has heart and fair minded people should know this.

Of course. But the church also has a face cold enough to justify the jibes. You see it in documents about inter-communion. In these, no matter how hard you try to understand the argument, you feel you've lost Christ before you reach the end.

Take the canon law about second unions. You know about the sacredness of marriage but you also know the sacredness of the new couple. You know their story doesn't match the Marriage Tribunal categories. You know how judged and rejected by the church they feel. Excluded from Communion. They feel trapped under the grid of law. So, is law the greatest of the virtues? Who says?

Many would claim to have seen a particularly cold face in the treatment of the child sexual abuse scandals. No one is saying it wasn't a terrible and complex thing to land on any bishop or superior's desk. Did the response have to be so messy, so hesitant, so open to allegations of cuteness? Again, the law and legal precautions seemed to call the shots.

This was tragic. When a church finds its response anywhere other than in the gospel, it is not only out of its depth – it is false to its mission. If we are to preach a gospel that is subversive, we ourselves should be the first to feel its winnowing force.

Style matters. It betrays attitude. That, in turn, indicates how well we have absorbed the mind of Christ. To the extent the church wears His face, she will be noted.

The institutional style

I'm deliberately talking about church as if it were solely the institution, capped by bishops, superiors, priests and religious. I believe it is here we find the reasons for the church's off-putting style.

Those reasons can be called clericalism. It is a caste system. Self-perpetuating. It doesn't feel it has to explain itself. It is about power. Essentially, it is a control system so it is ill at ease when questioned. Accountability is not favoured.

Clericalism rewards servility. It marginalises the independent. The resulting inbreeding weakens the stock.

Until recently, mystique protected clericalism from any kind of harsh analysis – a bit like the British Royal Family. All that has changed. The times demand quality in leadership. The harder it becomes to justify being identified with the church in our pressured culture, the more people committed to the church will want leadership to shape up, partly in better management skills but mainly in the insights of discipleship.

When clericalism has got us where we are, it is difficult to kick away the ladder along which we climbed. But not impossible. My deepest wish – and prayer – for church leaders is that they'd have more awareness of their own humanity and the decency of the people among whom they were reared. That they'd spend less time reading Roman documents and more time reading the wisdom of the people in their own place. That they'd cheer up.

Clericalism tries to dampen urgency by saying the church has seen all this many times before and survived. The fact is, it hasn't. Or clericalism blames the media for its troubles. Or a litany of plagues like materialism, secularism, relativism, individualism or hedonism. All the -isms in the dictionary. All except one. Its own virus. Clericalism.

Looking elsewhere

If clericalism is what is worst about the church, where it has led us is our best hope for the future. By that I mean the thinness of our leadership will force us to turn to lay people.

A priest I know works in an American diocese where they've been through it all. Long before the sexual scandals they were losing congregations. Believers were slipping away quietly, and doing so not necessarily because they had lost faith in God but because they had lost trust in the church.

As regards the young, they weren't switched *off* because they hadn't been switched *on* in the first place. They were into pop culture. It mightn't have much substance but at least it had life.

Women – married, divorced, single, religious – had their problems with the church. Priests were demoralised. Then came the scandals.

They were dark, ugly times. In desperation, the priests talked among themselves. They identified the problem as one of power, not theology. The abuse of power. They applied the same analysis to the problems that pre-dated the sexual scandals. Same thing. Abuse of power. They concluded that the gospel in their diocese was being warped by power.

They talked to their bishops. Straight talk. Together the bishops and priests hammered out statements on how they saw the situation. They put words on their helplessness.

The next step was to ask themselves, what now? Who to turn to? To the very people who seemed most disappointed in them. The laity.

They chiselled out sermons and newsletter articles, telling people how helpless they felt, asking forgiveness for their clericalism and asking for their help. Inviting lay people to phone, write or drop in to talk. They waited to see what would happen.

What happened was that many of the lay people did what the priests had done. They met privately first to hammer out their position. When they came they asked for two things. First, a guarantee that the invitation to help was genuine. Second, that they'd get some sort of training in their own roles and how to function in them.

The mood is different now. Many who walked away have stayed away. For the rest, there is new life.

I've spent some time in these parishes and it lifts the heart.

There is an air of coming into places that have been purged of something unhealthy. People seem happy in the new atmosphere. The clergy will admit to having been humbled but they are grateful that events have forced them out of a culture of power into one of co-operation. You can smell the hope and energy and it isn't all just American exuberance.

What is interesting is that these people will tell you it doesn't matter whether they or the priests are left- or right-wing, liberal or conservative. Where there is community, the dynamic works. If people feel their presence is respected and their point of view listened to, you get what researchers call 'high tension religion'. This is an energy build-up when different viewpoints meet in common cause.

At times, such energy will celebrate local social and moral trends. At other times it will be counter-culture and will challenge. At all times, it is alive, active and attempts to make the gospel work. What kills the spirit, they say, is timidity fed on fear.

Situations differ. But I believe there is a hint on how to handle our inadequate style of being church – and the virus of clericalism – in what those American parishes did.

A case of content

Earlier I said our problems were about content as well as style. Content is what style is meant to facilitate.

Content is about brain but not fully. Religion is as much about wonder as theology. About mystery, poetry, drama, music and ritual. About the cycle of the seasons and the heritage of devotions.

Much has been written recently about our Celtic heritage. I don't know enough about it to judge how much is historically accurate, how much is modern invention. Some accuse it of being 'a floating spirituality without the definiteness of faith'.

There is no denying that it touches something both deep and immediate in us as a people. Insights beyond words. We have talent enough to study it more, popularise what is solid and feed its parables into music, pageant and ritual.

Jubilee 2000 has potential for nourishing the soul. There is great hope in the emphasis on local heritage and local pilgrimage. The more we move ritual outdoors and recover the sacredness of where we live, the more attuned we may become to the sacredness of the eucharist and of those who gather to celebrate it.

The Jubilee can give us perspective, remind us of an older history and another people beneath the skin of where we now build roads, factories and homes.

The Media: friend, foe, neither?

Where would we be without having the media to blame for our troubles? No one will argue that we have perfect media, but then, who are we to throw stones? We talk about 'relationships with the media'. Our relationship is not with the media. It is with people through the media. Journalists' notebooks, cameras and microphones are not the end of the process. They provide us with a place where minds meet. Where we share the search.

The media are sometimes called the electronic pulpit. They are no such thing. A pulpit is a privileged place within an act of worship in the presence of believers. It proclaims the faith. It works under the assumption that we are there to celebrate faith.

With 'the media', you have no privilege, no selected audience. You can make no assumptions about common values or language. You are naked. This makes it a difficult place for clericalism and that is why I believe so many church people have such antipathy towards both the profession and the practice of media.

Today, the media are the main vehicle for debate and information. And so, the church – we all – dare not opt out of the forum they provide.

What more do we need to know about the importance of being there, of knowing the ground rules, of learning the language, of respecting the job of journalists, of how to tailor material to the occasion and the audience?

The media are part style, part content – attitudes as much as argument. This does not make them shallow, or a fit subject for suspicion.

A mature faith for a mature people

St Peter said we must be ready to give reasons for the faith that is in us. He was really making a plea for good religious education. Two thousand years later, we haven't quite got round to it.

Breandán Ó Madagáin has been Professor of Irish in NUIG. He studied for the priesthood at Maynooth. He left before being ordained. Those who were ordained had a fortieth reunion recently. They asked Breandán to speak to them.

He said the church avoids our hardest questions. If we are going to church, the presumption is that we have no problems with the existence of God, a next life or the claims of Jesus Christ. If we are not going, then the presumption is that we aren't interested. Wrong, on both counts.

The church, he said, has narrowed its agenda down to items like the scandals, the drop in vocations and our present moral confusion. But our big questions are about the fundamentals. God, Jesus Christ, the next life, Christ's resurrection and ours, the eucharist. These are treated as items of faith and the questions about them ignored. Faith may very well be the final stage but in the long search before faith, some intellectual support would be appreciated. It isn't there. As a result, struggling believers have no apparatus either to deal with their own questions or stand up to a critical barrage from those who choose to mock.

Breandán Ó Madagáin has identified a great need. What he is asking for is as much about intellectual honesty as it is about actual content – the sense of belonging to a church that is not afraid of questions.

Some of these questions will be doctrinal – like those about the existence of God and of a next life. Others will be moral – like attitudes to life in its coming and going and its quality in between. Other questions will be disciplinary – like celibacy or women priests (even though some insist this latter is doctrinal). And a final category of questions will ask about some of the stranger church customs – like indulgences and Mass stipends.

What I think is at stake here is not a demand for full answers or even the freedom to ask the questions. Rather, an acknowledgement that to have faith is automatically to have questions.

Somewhere I read that one of the councils talks about 'dark faith'. A good phrase. It honours doubt. The problem for the Christian is not the possibility of atheism or agnosticism. Both depend on having been let ask questions. The really scary thing is that as a believer you might be expected to get along without having any questions at all. Or having the freedom to ask them.

We are back to the importance of style.

Conclusion

Seamus Heaney's poem 'Scaffolding' is instructive:

> Masons, when they start upon a building,
> Are careful to test out the scaffolding;
>
> Make sure that planks won't slip at busy points,
> Secure all ladders, tighten bolted joints.
>
> And yet all this comes down when the job's done
> Showing off walls of sure and solid stone.
>
> So if, my dear, there sometimes seem to be
> Old bridges breaking between you and me
> Never fear. We may let the scaffolds fall
> Confident that we have built our wall.

The poem is about ripeness; about recognising when love invites into a new phase; about the moment of fretting as the old skin is shed and the beauty of what it has cradled is not quite yet revealed.

There may not be much obvious loveliness in what is exposed as the scaffolding is stripped from the church. But it is there. If we believe the resurrection story, beyond the shame there is new life. If only we can listen and learn from each other to know what to shed because it is ugly, and only scaffolding anyway. And if only we can listen and learn from each other what is of God and beautiful .

Why not leave the last word to Kavanagh:

> Under the flat flat grief of defeat
> Maybe hope is the seed.

The Church in the New Millennium

✠ *Willie Walsh*

As I grew up in the 1940s and 50s I often wondered if I could possibly live to see the end of the century. The magical year 2000 seemed so far away. I wondered too what the world and indeed what I myself might be like at that point. It goes without saying that the pictures conjured up in that exercise of the imagination would have been very different from the actual reality which is now upon us.

We approach the end of a millennium, the end of a century, the end of a decade. It is natural to look back, to remember, to try to learn from the past. It is natural to look forward to try to influence the future.

End of a millennium

We approach the end of the second millennium which began with the great divide of the Christian Church between East and West, a divide which sadly persists to this day. Mid-way through that same millennium we had further major divisions of the Western Church into several denominations, which divisions have sadly multiplied over the years. Despite these divisions the Christian churches contributed very significantly to the progress of practically every aspect of civilisation in the West, whether it be education or the arts, whether it be science or engineering, agriculture or medicine. And how can we measure the contributions of monks and martyrs, of philosophers and mystics, and of ordinary people whose faith inspired all that is best in humanity?

End of a century

We approach the end of a century in which the Roman Catholic Church became more centralised and more disciplined in its structure and its practice. The first half of the century in particular saw a growth in a disciplined Irish church, secure in its own rightness and righteousness. The rapid advances made by the Catholic Church in the United States and the new world generally, the heroic work of so many of our missionaries in Africa and elsewhere, the growing number of young people who devoted their lives to priesthood and religious life, and the almost universal attendance to religious obligations and practices by the people, gave a confidence and authority to the Catholic Church in Ireland. That confidence led it at times to think it had the right answers to all questions, be they ecclesiastical or political, be they educational or social. The church was indeed the dominant influence in Irish society and at times used that influence in a clumsy manner.

The many hurts caused by that dominant church are to be deeply regretted. It would, however, be less than generous or indeed truthful not to recognise too the contribution made by the church, especially in the fields of education and medicine and indeed in the daily lives of ordinary people.

The 1960s brought new hopes, new vision of change. The much loved Pope John XXIII 'opened the windows of the Vatican' and called an Ecumenical Council. Vatican II gave a new vision of church as people of God in contrast to the previous strongly clerical church. It spoke in a new way about Christian unity, about dialogue with non-Christian religions, about the dignity of each person's conscience, about principles of religious freedom.

There was of course an air of newness in the sixties. John Kennedy became the first Catholic President of the US, Harold Macmillan spoke of 'winds of change blowing through Africa', Sean Lemass visited Northern Ireland to meet Terence O'Neill, and the 'angry young men' committed themselves to changing the world.

However, not all the new hopes raised by Vatican II were to be fulfilled. Indeed the first major crisis of the century in the teaching authority of the church came in the second half of the

60s with the publication of *Humanae Vitae* which upheld the traditional teaching of the church in regard to contraception. For the first time, large numbers of Catholic couples not only felt they could not follow the church teaching but many began to question the very validity of the teaching itself.

Gradually, through the 70s and 80s, other traditional positions of the church were subjected to questioning – in particular in the areas of sexuality and marriage. This perhaps was the beginning of what is sometimes called 'à la carte' Catholicism where many,while professing adherence to the Catholic faith, at the same time reject or ignore some of its official teachings.

End of a decade

These difficulties, however, were insignificant in comparison to what was to happen in the 90s. A series of scandals involving priests and religious revealed themselves. In particular the revelation that priests and religious had abused children in their care brought a real sense of pain and shame to all who had the concerns of church at heart. The fact that the most of this abuse had occurred at a time when the church in Ireland appeared to be at its strongest raised serious doubts about how we measured the strength or perhaps the health of that church. The perception that religious, and in particular bishops, might have engaged in some sort of cover up of the abusers aroused a lot of anger.

Not all of the anger directed towards the church in recent years, however, is about sexual abuse. I believe that much of that anger comes from past hurts inflicted by church personnel at a time when it wasn't easy to question the conduct of priest or religious. Now that it is permissible to criticise the church, many hurts from the past are being given voice. I do believe that the opportunity to give voice to such past hurts is a healthy and a healing one.

Signs of darkness

Going hand in hand with the revelation of scandals of the 90s there has been a significant fall off in religious practice, although that decline was already under way in the previous decade.

- Our Sunday Mass attendance has fallen from high 80 per cent to low 60 per cent, with much greater falls in the larger centres of population.
- There has been the virtual disappearance of confession in many areas.
- Family prayer has for most families become a rarity.
- Vocations to priesthood and religious life have fallen dramatically and there are no hopeful signs of an upturn.
- A significant percentage of Catholics reject/question the teaching of the church on matters such as family planning, divorce, interchurch eucharistic sharing, etc.

Signs of light

It is easy to list the signs of darkness in our church as we approach the new millennium. There is much talk of a church in crisis.

It is important that we don't lose our nerve. The church has been in crisis before and has recovered. There is no reason to believe that the Spirit of God is any less active and alive in today's church than in the early church. Where that Spirit may be leading us at this time is not easy to discern. We can only pray that each one of us may be open to, and may have the courage and the generosity to be inspired by, the Spirit. It would indeed appear that we will have to reconcile ourselves to a period of some uncertainty in the church going into the new century.

And if we can list the signs of darkness we can also list some signs of light:

- At a time of increasing national prosperity there is a growing awareness that material prosperity is not satisfying the needs of the whole person.
- There is a growing sense of the brotherhood and sisterhood of mankind and of the profound dignity of each individual person.
- There is an increased quest for a deeper understanding of faith among many of the laity, with a real interest in linking spirituality and life.
- There is a strong sense that the Jubilee 2000 provides us with an opportunity for new life and new growth in the church.

- There is an emerging consensus that the church has made many mistakes in the past and that we need to acknowledge these wrong doings and ask pardon for them.
- There is a significant willingness on the part of people to become involved in their local church and to take ownership of their church.

Ultimately our hope is Jesus Christ himself who promised that he would be with us always. Death and resurrection were central to the life of Christ – death and new life will continue to be central to our church.

A Christ-centred church

Our hope indeed is in Jesus Christ. If the very mission of the church is to continue the work of Christ, then it must be always inspired by the life and teaching of Jesus Christ. There is no getting away from the life and teaching of Jesus Christ. This is essentially what separates the church from the many new age movements. Much of what the new age philosophy proposes is worthy of respect but it lacks what must always be the heart and the core of our faith, namely that Jesus Christ came to bring salvation, to restore us to friendship with God through his life and teaching, through his death and resurrection. All that we teach in the name of the church must be tested and measured against the life and teaching of Jesus Christ. All that we practice in the name of the church must be measured against the life and teaching of Jesus Christ.

A church of the people

In July 1998 the parish priest of Killanena, a small parish in East Clare, was moved to another parish. He was not replaced by a resident priest. The announcement came as a shock to the people of the parish. I was invited to a public meeting attended by more than half of the total population. I was told in a courteous but most forthright manner of their disappointment, their hurt and their anger. I had talked a lot as bishop about consultation. Yet when it came to a decision which affected their lives so deeply I had failed totally to do any consultation. I apologised for my failure to consult and tried to reassure them that a priest would always be available to carry out all duties for which a priest is required.

Twelve months later a representative group from the parish approached me to say that they felt they no longer needed a full-time priest – they were happy about what had been happening over the past year and wanted to continue with the model of church which was emerging.

The Killanena model is not prefect and the people of Killanena wouldn't want to make that claim. There are still a small number of people who are not happy with the arrangements. I believe, however, that what has happened is that the people of Killanena have now a far greater sense of ownership of their church and parish than they had in the past. It is their church, their parish. They – through various sub-committees of their parish council – have taken responsibility for the physical plant, the finances, the liturgy, care of the elderly, faith development, etc.

Vatican II emphasised that the church is the people of God. I believe that one of the great challenges before us as we enter the new century is to facilitate that understanding of church. For too long as clergy we have 'said Mass' for the people, we have 'given them the sacrament', we have 'told them' how they should live their lives. It is not because we are getting older as priests, it is not because there are fewer of us, that we should facilitate people in taking ownership of their own local church. Getting older and fewer may, however, in the Lord's own way, be the occasion which will enable the local church to become truly the people of God.

An authentic church

To speak of the church as authentic is open to a wide variety of interpretations. When I suggest that the church in the new millennium must always strive to be authentic, I have in mind that it must be real, it must ring true to people's lives. I am not suggesting for a moment that it should in some way adopt its teaching to the values by which people live. I am suggesting, however, that it must in some way relate to the actual lives that people live.

I have difficulty if I hear priest or bishop talking about the blessing that a handicapped child can be to a family when some families find the caring for a handicapped child an enormous burden on their daily lives.

I have difficulty if I hear priest or bishop speak of people who too easily walk out of marriage when my limited experience tells me that, for the vast majority of people whose marriage has broken up, the break up has only come after years of deep pain and suffering.

I have difficulty if we speak too easily about the faith of the Irish people while not recognising that so many of those whom I would regard as committed Catholics are really struggling with their beliefs right now.

I have difficulty with simple slogans which tell parents that all will be well if they pray and act responsibly when I know so many parents, who have genuinely done their best in trying to hand on the faith to their children, now find that their children reject that faith and practice.

When I speak of an authentic church, I have in mind a church which recognises that, for many people in today's world, trying to live their lives in accordance with Christian teaching can be a real struggle. Perhaps we might speak of a struggling church.

A struggling church

I believe that one of the most hopeful happenings in recent times has been the developing theology which reminds us that we are a pilgrim church, with priests and people walking together on our journey towards God, struggling together on our journey towards God.

My generation of priests were nourished on a spirituality which gave us the impression that a priest ought to be perfect – well nearly perfect anyway. I suspect that many of us, realising that we were far from perfect, felt that it was 'only me' who was so weak. It was still alright to expect others to be perfect without acknowledging the struggle it is for all of us to live up to Christ's teaching in our lives.

Do some older priests remember St Thomas' *'bonum ex integra causa, malum ex quocumque defectu'*, which we interpreted as 'to be good you must be good in every aspect of life, to be bad it is sufficient to be bad in any single area'. Simplistic? Yes, but somehow I feel it left us with little appreciation of the real goodness within ourselves and within others and too great a consciousness of our inadequacies.

Christ was never severe on the 'sinner', the one who failed through human weakness. He was severe on the ones who condemned others – 'woe to you who place heavy burdens on others' shoulder …' I worry at times what he may be telling us who are in positions of authority in the church.

When I speak of a struggling church, I have in mind too the need to recognise that so many people in today's church have difficulties with a number of areas of teaching, such as that in respect to family planning, clerical celibacy, exclusion of people in second unions from full eucharistic participation, interchurch sharing of eucharist, etc.

One of the primary obligations of a bishop is 'to preach and teach the faith to be believed and to be put into practice in life according to the Word of God and the magisterium of the church'. (Synod of European Bishops II, *Lineamenta*) It is an obligation which I take very seriously. I have difficulty, however, in placing certain teachings outside the area of discussion. To suggest that certain positions of the church may not be discussed runs the risk of being accused of lack of confidence in the reasoning supporting them. Institutional authority of the church alone is not sufficient to convince people of the truth of the Catholic faith. We need to continue to study, to examine and to re-examine the reasons on which these teachings are based, and hopefully to find improved ways of presenting them.

A repentant church

In speaking about the Jubilee, the Holy Father has referred on a number of occasions to the importance of reconciliation. 'The church should become more fully conscious of the sinfulness of her children, recalling those times in history when they departed

from the spirit of Christ and his gospel.' (*Tertio Millennio,* 33)
Among the sins of the past that we need to acknowledge and to
ask pardon for, the Pope lists:

i. The painful reality of division among Christians.

ii. The acceptance of intolerance and even use of violence
supposedly in the service of truth.

iii. Failures to defend human rights.

iv. Responsibility shared by many Christians for grave forms
of injustice and exclusion.

Perhaps each country, diocese and even parish might do well
to complete the list for themselves.

I believe we need to acknowledge and to ask pardon for the
hurts caused to:

i. People who have been abused sexually or indeed physically
and emotionally. I am not thinking here just of abuse done by
priests or religious – I am thinking of abuse done by any person claiming to belong to our church.

ii. Women who feel that their role in the church has been constantly under-valued.

iii. People whose marriages have broken down and who now
feel excluded because they have entered a second union. And
can I add the often forgotten ones – the spouses who are left
behind in their aloneness while many plead for those who
have gone on to these second unions.

iv. People of other Christian denominations hurt by what
they have seen as our intolerant stand on interchurch marriages and other areas.

v. Politicians and other public figures who have taken perhaps a different view on political, social and religious issues.
I have especially in mind politicians on the left of the political
spectrum.

vi. Poor people who have felt, and often justly felt, that the
church has not stood close to them. There was no ambiguity
about where Christ stood.

vii. People whose lives have been tormented by scruples
which may have arisen by our misunderstanding of sexuality.

viii. People who feel excluded because of their sexual orient-
ation.

It may sound like an old time confession – attempting to as-
semble an impressive list for the priest. The reality is, however,
that there are a lot of people who have been hurt. And which of
us can put our hand on our heart and say 'I have made no contribution whatever to any of these hurts'? If you can, then good for
you; if you can't, then join us in asking for forgiveness. It will
surely do a little to restore justice and it will help the healing
process.

A challenging church
We approach the millennium at a time of unprecedented prosperity in Ireland. The Celtic tiger roars on. 'We never had it so
good' might be the signature tune. It would be churlish in the
extreme not to recognise and give credit for the good job that has
been done by workers, employers, politicians, etc., in overcom-
ing the serious economic difficulties of the past.

It would be equally churlish to fail to recognise that while
most of us have benefited by that progress, many too have been
left behind. In a climate of aggressive individualism many individuals are simply unable to cope. I think of the long-term unemployed – some perhaps at this stage simply incapable without specialised help to cope with a job. I think of the 15.3 per cent
of the population recently ranked by the UN Human Poverty
Index as 'living in human poverty'. The same survey classified
us as having one of the highest 'child poverty' rates in Europe.

A church which tries to be faithful to the teaching of Christ
must constantly be challenging all forms of injustice wherever
they exist.

The ultimate challenge, however, will continue to be the
great commandment of love. The early Christians were recognised by their love for each other. What a wonderful challenge
for the church in the new millennium?

The Contributors

DENIS CARROLL is an historian and theologian. His publications include *Land: An Issue for the Millennium* (1998) and *Unusual Suspects: Twelve Radical Clergy* (1998).

THE MOST REVEREND RICHARD CLARKE is Bishop of Meath and Kildare. A noted historian, his contribution on sectarianism to the Church of Ireland Synod (1999) has received wide acclaim. He is a contributor to another set of millennium essays, *A Time to Build* (APCK, 1999).

GABRIEL DALY, an Augustinian priest, teaches theology in Trinity College Dublin. He has written extensively on relating Christian faith to the modern world. His *Creation and Redemption* (1987) has become a classic work in the theology of creation.

MICHAEL DRUMM is a priest of the Elphin diocese. He teaches theology at Mater Dei Institute, Dublin, and has lectured widely on the place of religion in Irish society. His *Passage to Pasch* was published by The Columba Press in 1998.

JOHN DUNLOP is a former Moderator of the Presbyterian Church in Ireland and author of *A Precarious Kind of Belonging*. He is Minister of Rosemary Presbyterian Church, Belfast.

ROBERT DUNLOP is Pastor of Brannockstown Baptist Church in Co Kildare. A noted broadcaster, he is author of many historical and theological articles. Active in reconciliation work, his collection of poems, *Pathways to Peace,* was published in 1998.

DONAL FLANAGAN is a theologian, broadcaster and reviewer. Alongside his theological specialism, he is currently involved in historico-cultural projects in Wicklow and Wexford.

DERMOT KEOGH is Professor of History in NUI Cork. His extensive writings on modern Irish history include a history of the Jewish community in Ireland. Dr Keogh's analysis is central to *Building Trust in Ireland,* studies commissioned by the Forum For Peace and Reconciliation (1996).

COLM KILCOYNE is a priest of the archdiocese of Tuam and is parish priest of Cong, Co Mayo. For years he wrote a column in the *Sunday Tribune.* Widely known for plain speaking on church matters, he lectures at clergy conferences and diocesan retreats.

JOSEPH LIECHTY is a Mennonite who for many years has been involved in peace studies. He has written extensively on ecumenism. Currently, he works with the Irish School of Ecumenics' project 'Moving Beyond Sectarianism'.

SEÁN MAC RÉAMOINN is a broadcaster and writer whose books include *Vatacáin II agus an Réabhlóid Chultúrtha* (1987) and *Laylines: Partial Views of Church and Society* (1997). He has edited four titles in the *Columba Explorations* series (1995-1998) and *The Pleasures of Gaelic Poetry* (Allen Lane, 1982). He writes a monthly column, 'Laylines', in *Doctrine and Life.*

THE MOST REVEREND WILLIE WALSH is Bishop of Killaloe. His emphasis on bringing the church closer to people's lives has been welcomed not only in his own diocese but across the country.